REAL ESTATE
FOR THE GENERATIONS

REAL ESTATE
FOR THE GENERATIONS

A Family Team Guiding You Through Real Estate

STEVE, LOYAL AND RICK
MESSERSCHMIDT

To order additional copies of this book, contact:
Xlibris Corporation
1-888-795-4274
www.Xlibris.com
Orders@Xlibris.com
58000

CONTENTS

Dedication

We have written this book to be a quick-guide for all your real estate needs. Whether you are buying, selling, or investing, you can count on this book to be your reference and source of knowledge.

*This book is dedicated to the most important people in our business—you. To all of our past, current, and future clients, we want to say **Thank You**. We appreciate your business, friendship, and trust. This book is for you.*

Foreword

I am blessed to have studied for countless hours with innovative thinkers from all parts of the world and to have been introduced to many different businesses and life philosophies. I have encountered ideas and methods guaranteed to empower individuals to build global business empires. High volumes of concepts and strategies have been proven to improve the quality of one's life. The more I learn, the more I realize how much I do not know. Continuous learning is both empowering and humbling.

If there is one fundamental success factor that I have learned, however, it is the absolute inescapable truth that nothing truly great happens without the silent, but undeniable power of teamwork. Something wonderful occurs when people who are united through shared values come together with a common purpose.

I'm sure you have no doubt about the great works that effective teamwork can bring about. But like all great things in life, they don't come without tremendous effort. It is a difficult task to bring a team together, and a completely different and increasingly challenging task to build business models and sustainable action patterns that will keep that team working at the highest level possible. Very few teams actually make this dynamic work. Only a select few individuals can complete the difficult task of relinquishing their need for recognition, surrendering their own ideas and ego when needed, and harmonizing their goals with one another to produce unparalleled service for the customer.

Yes, it is true that this only happens on rare occasions, so when it does, you feel blessed to be involved with the team that makes it happen. For this reason, I am honored and grateful to write the foreword for The Messerschmidt Team and their highly anticipated book, *Real Estate for the Generations*. Many groups claim to be a team, but The Messerschmidt Team is a truly effective team that has the highly complicated and every changing game of real estate figured out. This team gets RESULTS.

Loyal, Rick, and Steve are, without question, servant leaders. Bottom line—they have the total package. They have a clear vision they are working toward every day that keeps them progressively and aggressively improving their skills and knowledge. They possess the determination and decisive commitment to service that was alive when this country was established by our Founding Fathers. And The Messerschmidt Team has a calmness and upbeat attitude that makes them *fun* to work with.

I personally observed the hard work and intense thought that was put into this book by the team over the past several months. There were many times when they could have put this book on the back burner and focused on other things, but they persisted. They knew this book would educate people in Sioux Falls and empower them to make wise decisions at the right times. That was their motivation for this book and it is the reason why The Messerschmidt Team, year after year, remains one of the highest producing teams in the entire Midwest.

Whether you are a first time homebuyer, an investor, or looking to sell your home for the first or fifth time, *Real Estate for the Generations* is a must-have. Your bookshelf is not complete without it. I suggest you read it, re-read it, and pay it forward by giving a few copies away to family and close friends.

Jeremy D Brown
Author of *No Limit Living: How to Think Big, Act Bold and Live with Purpose*

Loyal Messerschmidt has enjoyed a long and highly successful real estate career with over 32 years of experience in the Sioux Falls market. Loyal specializes in residential real estate and new construction as a Certified Residential Specialist (CRS).

Through all his years of experience in the real estate industry, Loyal has remained committed to continuing his education, and has established himself as an authority figure in the Sioux Falls area in real estate. Many agents—new and seasoned—seek out Loyal to receive the advice and knowledge that Loyal happily shares.

In 2006, Loyal was awarded the Realtor's Choice Award. This is a significant achievement due to the fact that the recipient is chosen by Loyal's peers as the REALTOR® they prefer to work with.

Loyal has been married to his wife Judy for over 49 years. Real estate truly is a family affair with the Messerschmidts, with two of three sons—Rick and Steve—being REALTORS®. His third son, Dan, works as a general manager of Sioux Printing, overseeing more than 60 employees.

Loyal brings a real sense of experience and confidence to all his transactions and clients. He enjoys his business and has truly made his mark on the industry on both a local and regional level.

After 49 years of marriage, over 32 years in real estate, and now living in his 24th home, Loyal is still going stronger than ever, but has decided to cut back a bit to a 50-hour work week.

"We really appreciated your help in every aspect of selling our previous home and buying our new home. Thank you very much for everything Loyal!! There was no way we could have done it without your help!"
Bob and Diane Biver

Direct: 605-274-7226
Email: team@messerschmidtrealty.com

Steve Messerschmidt has over 25 years of experience assisting buyers and sellers in Sioux Falls and the surrounding areas. In 2002, Steve was given the highly sought after and distinguished South Dakota Realtor of The Year Award.

He served as president of the Sioux Falls Board of Realtors from 2000-2001, where he was the Sioux Falls Board of Realtors Realtor of the Year in 2001.

He has served as the Secretary, Treasurer, Vice President, and President of the Realtors of the Sioux Empire, as well as being the South Dakota State Director. He served on the Administrative Committee of the State Board of Directors as well as on the Government Affairs Committee of the State Board of Directors. Steve has also served for nine years on the board for Family Services, which counsels families in need through crisis situations. In addition to all of his dedicated service, Steve serves as a board member of the Evangelical Lutheran Good Samaritan Society.

Steve's educational advancement is a priority in his career, and he has participated in the SDAR Leadership Conference and NAR Leadership Summit. Thanks to his countless hours of training, study, and experience, Steve has received the CRS Designation.

Steve serves the Sioux Falls community with pride and enthusiasm while also enjoying a wonderful family life with his wife Kim, daughter Danielle and son Drew. To Steve, making time for his family is equally as important as making time for his business.

"We are quite pleased with Steve's services in both purchasing and selling our home. His professionalism extended beyond our expectations and beyond our previous experiences in buying and selling four homes in the last 20 years."
Howard and Gloria Burmester

Cell: 605-366-6838
Direct: 605-274-7217
Email: *steve@messerschmidtrealty.com*

14

Rick Messerschmidt brings a new enthusiasm and unique experience to The Messerschmidt Team with his 11 years of experience selling real estate in Phoenix, AZ. He has extensive experience and is highly specialized in Residential and New Construction Homes. Rick has various certifications and designations, including:

- CRS—Certified Residential Specialist
- GRI—Graduate of Real Estate Institute
- RCC—Residential Construction Certified
- CNHS—Certified New Home Specialist

Aside from his successful real estate career, Rick also enjoys spending time with his wife Cheryl, his two daughters Samantha and Allison, his two stepdaughters Ashleigh and Tera, his stepson Ryan, and his stepgranddaughter Marleigh. Rick takes great pride in both his clients and his family.

"We have never done business with an agent so thorough, honest, and upbeat. Even though I'm sure you were busy you made us feel like we were your first priority. I would recommend Rick to anyone."
Colin & Kirsten Doherty

Cell: 605-553-1129
Direct: 605-274-7263
Email: *rick@messerschmidtrealty.com*

For Sellers

"The entire process was expertly handled and considering the fact that only two people looked at the house and then it sold speaks for itself. The closing was painless and the purchase of the new home was perfect. No issues or problems. Thanks a Million!"
Bob And Mary Jane Melcher

There are three critical reasons why you should use a REALTOR® when selling your home:

- Representation
- Marketing
- Negotiation

It is not just important to have an expert to guide you through today's ever complicating selling process—it is vital. Knowing there is a professional watching out for your best interests is like knowing your car is going to start every morning: one less thing to worry about.

One of the most important assets in one's life is time. How you spend your time is a key factor to living a fulfilling life. A full time REALTOR®, like each member of The Messerschmidt Team, will work 24-7 to sell your home, which allows you to spend your time on the most important things like your family and lifestyle.

There are many technical issues that must be considered when selling real estate in South Dakota, federal and state mandated laws and forms being just a few of them. There is an enormous amount of paperwork that needs to be done and done correctly. The Messerschmidt Team will help to relieve the stress and hassle of your transaction. Simply put, we make it significantly easier for you.

We always represent you and your best interest throughout the entire transaction. When you are working with The Messerschmidt Team, you have access to one of the greatest marketing tools for the sale of your home—Multiple Listing Service (MLS). With the aid of the MLS, your home is viewed by thousands of other REALTORS® who are working with buyers eager to find the right home.

"Loyal was very quick in getting the information onto the MLS system which is why I think our house sold so quickly. He gave all the information to us in a timely manner, and sound advice to effectively sell our house."
Thomas Falconer

The Messerschmidt Team wants to make the sale of your home a noisy one! When we say noisy we are talking about letting as many people know about your home as possible. This creates many more opportunities to find the right buyer for your home. We know that the right buyer for your home is the person who likes your home the best and will pay the most for it.

The National Association of REALTORS® tells us that 94% of buyers start their home search first on the internet (www.realtor.org). When you work with us, we market your home on numerous websites, some of which are accessible only to our sellers.

We have a vested interest in the sale of your home. Your success is our success. We are full time REALTORS®, and we are solely focused on the sale of your home and achieving your real estate goals.

We have a complete marketing program that is proven to be highly effective and researched diligently to offer you the best and most exclusive marketing opportunities for the sale of your home.

"The best way out is always through."
—Robert Frost

We will negotiate the best possible price and terms for your home; in fact, this is where we excel.

As a professional real estate team, we take the emotion out of the selling process. When you are emotionally attached to the circumstance, it is almost impossible to step back and see the big picture. We are able to look at all the angles to a problem and guide you to a successful outcome. After all, *you can't see the entire picture if you are in the frame.*

The Messerschmidt Team will come and look at your home objectively, comparing it to other similar properties that have sold or not sold in your area. We specialize in getting you all the latest market information so the correct price can be set on your home.

Through our 68 years of combined experience, we have found there are five key factors that go into the sale of your home: 1) Price and Time, 2) Condition, 3) Location, 4) Financing terms, and 5) Realtors. To make this a useful book for you, we will list them and explain each in detail. We have also arranged this book according to common questions we receive while serving our clients. For each of the five key factors listed, we will answer all the common questions related to each factor. Think of this as a Real Estate FAQ for the sale of your home.

"Try not to become a man of success, but a man of value."
—Albert Einstein

1. Price and Time

"What will my home sell for and how long will it take?"

This is a great question. The higher you price you house over-market, the longer the time it will take to get your house sold. Not only that, but the longer it will take to find a buyer to make an offer, the lower the sale price. You never want your home to be market worn, because buyers and REALTORS® will ask, *"What is wrong with that house?"*

This is extremely important, because a house that is priced competitively will sell faster and has a greater possibility of having more than one offer. A seller typically gets their best price in the early stages of selling their home. After that, the activity goes down significantly. This is why we market your home strategically and with massive action to get you a buyer in the early stages so you can get top dollar.

"Loyal got us an offer in less than 24 hours and without a single open house. Loyal knows real estate and was completely honest with us about every little detail. Very trustworthy. He came to us when we needed to meet. He and his staff took care of every little detail and we didn't have to worry about a thing. I would definitely use his services again."
Nancy Potts

Understand that when your home comes on the market, there are buyers who have been looking in that area and that price range. When all of these people have viewed your home and have not made an offer, then we have to wait for a new group of buyers to come into the market place. In this case, sellers effectively clear out the buyers in their price range by pricing their home higher than the competition.

In our experience, we have found that normally the first offer is the best offer. The first buyer is usually the buyer who likes it the most, moves the quickest, and will pay the most for it. We would go as far as saying that nine out of ten times, the first offer is the best offer in a stable or slightly increasing market (like Sioux Falls).

We've seen a seller turn down an offer, then proceed to contact us weeks later telling us that they would accept the offer when the buyer has already brought another property. This is why The Messerschmidt Team, with our experience and understanding of these circumstances, can guide you and the buyer down the path of agreement where the end outcome and time frame is best for all parties.

"We really appreciate how fast our house sold and how easy it was for us to buy a new house. Thank you so much."
George Lee

Ever-Changing Market

"What is the real estate market like today?"

You always want to keep in mind that the market is ever-changing from week to week. A major advantage to using The Messerschmidt Team is that we will keep you informed of the local market as it changes. The number of properties currently coming onto the market, as well as the number of properties being sold or removed because they did not sell, will continue to change your home's market position. This puts more price pressure on your property during a downward phase in the market because more competition exists. On the other hand, when more properties are selling, this creates less competition, which could aid in the property selling quickly and closer to the original asking price.

However, even in a stable market, you still need to beat your competition. The Messerschmidt Team will help you get the best results under all market conditions.

"Thanks for your help in selling our former home. We appreciate your suggestions to assist in getting it sold in spite of the saturated market and rising interest rates."
Susan Elgersma

When evaluating property, some REALTORS® use only one method of determining the market price of your home—they only look at houses that have sold. Based on our experience, we have identified five proven methods to help you determine the market price of your home.

2. Condition: What Buyers are Looking For

"Do I have to do anything to my home to sell it?"

You only get one chance to make a first impression

It is essential to keep in mind that as a buyer is looking at your home, they are looking for reasons why they should not buy your home. Once they find the reason, whether it is price or condition, they are gone, and more than likely they are not coming back. That is why it is essential to have your home in top showing condition to beat your competition.

"The difference between a successful person and others is not a lack of strength, not a lack of knowledge, but rather a lack in will."
Vince Lombardi

We help sellers to evaluate their home, with all the positive and negative features, and relate these factors to a balance scale.

The scale above represents all the negative and positive factors of your home, those that will help and those that will hinder its sale. The two must balance. If the property has numerous repairs needed, this will tip the scale negatively in the buyer's opinion. In order to bring the scale back into balance your property needs something unique and special. There must be a near perfect balance between all negative and positive factors of your home. Price and condition must also balance.

"Steve gave us an honest assessment of our house and then worked hard to sell it. We value Steve's judgment and expertise. We highly recommend Steve to those who are buying or selling a house in the Sioux Falls market."
Brain and Patti Moberly

A good example to illustrate how this balance works would be homes in the historical districts. These properties typically need updating, but they are still popular for the simple fact that buyers want to be in that location. There are limited options for buyers in that location, thus the scales balance out.

Think of a lakefront property home. This type of property is a finite product. If a buyer wants a home of this type, they just buy it. It is not about the home; it is about the location and lifestyle. Thus, the scale balances itself out.

This scale applies to all types of properties, including acreages. The scale balances because acreage properties are very unique and hard to find. Even though the property may need a lot of repairs the buyers tend to be forgiving because there are so few to choose from. It is all about balance, and we have this balancing act down to a science.

As we said before, when a buyer goes through a list of potential properties, at first they are not looking for their home—they are eliminating homes. Their main purpose is to find reasons to eliminate homes on the list and get the search narrowed down to just a few homes. We consider what buyers look for to ensure your house stays in the running.

Properties that are in a better condition than the competition sell in a shorter amount of time and for a higher price. The buyers are comparing your home to the competition at all times. They are looking at the condition and features of your home and directly relating it to the other possible properties. There is an epic battle between your home and the home next door.

What features do buyers consider? This completely depends on the buyer's needs and wants, but some of the features buyers compare between your property and the competition, listed in no particular order, are:

- Location
- Bedrooms
- Baths
- Kitchens
- Garage
- Square footage
- Main floor laundry
- Fireplace
- Type of woodwork
- Siding
- Windows
- Yard (fenced, non-fenced, or sprinkler system)

Each buyer has different needs and wants when looking for a home which are completely unique. For example, some buyers will only buy a home with a triple car garage. Some buyers will want a big kitchen while others won't care at all. Yet a home with a big kitchen will be priced higher than one that has a small kitchen because it appeals to a higher percentage of buyers. This can be a complicated and confusing process, but we take care of it for you.

Buyers pay close attention to a home's floor plan. A few reasons we have found most buyers walk away from a home can be classified under the title of functional obsolescence/bad floor plan:

- Kitchens in the lower level and not on the main floor
- Small eating areas or no eating area for the family
- Too big of a house on too small of a lot—we have found it is better to have a nice, small house on a big lot
- Windows that look out into your neighbor's house
- Dining room too far from the kitchen
- Pet odors
- Smoking odors and stains
- Not clean
- No sparkle

After spending a small time viewing homes with any of these problems, buyers walk away.

Curb Appeal

"What's wrong with my curb?"

You have about 30 seconds to make a favorable impression on a buyer. If any negative aspects are displayed or noticed within this time frame, buyers will eliminate your house permanently from their list. We have had buyers who will pull up to the house and not even get out of the car because of lack of curb appeal.

Curb appeal is your first and biggest impression to a prospective buyer. Especially with approximately 94% of buyers searching for homes on the internet.

Question: what do they see on the internet while searching for homes? They see a picture of the front of the house or Internet Curb Appeal.

The average buyer will drive by your home without the REALTOR® initially and we all know there is only one chance for a first impression. The first time they look at the home, whether in person, in a picture, or on the internet, they will make an irrevocable decision to eliminate the home from their possibilities within seconds. If the buyer notices needed repairs, they will wonder what else is wrong with the property. *We cannot stress enough the significance the curb appeal has on the sale of your home.*

Now that they've gotten out of the car and are approaching the front door, you are over the first hurdle. What we will help you do is view your home through a buyer's eyes. Always remember, they are looking for reasons to eliminate your home.

Any negative impressions as they come up to the front door will set their state of mind for the entire viewing. If they see something negative, they will begin to focus on and look for other negative items in the home for the remainder of the viewing.

If this happens, they enter the home with a negative mindset and not the positive one we want. This is not a simple process. Leave it to us. We have done this literally thousands of times. As a matter of fact, we have done it over 2,900 times.

Buyers buy homes on emotion. You need to understand that one of our jobs is to get the buyer emotionally attached to your home, and then help them intellectually justify the purchase of it.

Since people buy homes on emotion and then justify the purchase on facts, here are some facts that they will consider:

- Proximity to shopping, school, and work
- No repairs needed on the home
- Good interest rate and payments
- Amount of storage space
- Kitchen quality and size

Emotional reasons a buyer will purchase a home may include:

- Family can grow old here
- Other family members close
- Look of the house
- Colors of the home inside and outside
- Feel of the home
- Smell of the home
- Lifestyle

"The time is always right to do what is right."
Martin Luther King, Jr.

The only way to reach a buyer's emotions is to effect their physical senses. We recommend to our clients that during showings they set the atmosphere of their home so the experience will affect all the physical senses: seeing, hearing, smelling, tasting, and touching.

Remember, when you work with us, we tell you exactly what you need to do inside and out to get your home market ready. We will tell you what you need to hear, not just what you want to hear.

"Our greatest glory is not in never falling but in rising every time we fall."
Confucius

3. Location

The location of your home is, most often, the number one factor that affects sales price. Location obviously affects the price by the desirability of the location itself. A good location will have a positive effect on the price and an undesirable location will have a negative effect on the price.

While a good location will sell much easier than an undesirable location, buyers have diverse needs for varying locations. Whether a location is a positive or a negative will depend of the buyer's needs and wants. What may be a positive for one buyer will be a negative for another.

The Messerschmidt Team can help you to determine how location impacts the sales price of your home. Even though you, as the seller, have lived in that house and may not be thinking about the location as being necessarily negative or positive, we think in terms of the buyer's wants and needs. These needs change dramatically according to each buyer. Our experience has helped us gain accurate knowledge as to what some of the major considerations are that you need to be aware of relating to location. Even though you as a seller cannot control any of these aspects, it will benefit you to be aware of these considerations.

School Areas

This is the number one criterion that buyers with children look for in their next home, given that many parents love to watch their kids walk to school.

Usually, this is a non-negotiable factor for buyers. Most of the time they will also not be willing to move their children out of their current school district, as many parents find this is too much of a change for the children.

On the other hand, buyers who do not have children typically don't want to live across the street from a school. This is because of too much traffic happening just before and after school. Frequently, buyers ask to be several blocks from schools.

Shopping

Some buyers want to be closer to malls and major shopping locations for convenience. Other buyers want to be as far away as they can be from such areas, though they are in the minority. The location of a seller's home can be a major benefit if it is a time saver for the buyer.

Parks

Virtually everyone likes to be close to parks. We have found this to be an added bonus to most buyers, as it gives them a secondary backyard to enjoy. Being close to a park can add zest and liveliness to the property and will attract buyers with active lifestyles.

Access to Interstate or Highway

This aspect will make it much easier for buyers who have a commute to work. By having easy access to major through-streets, this saves driving time to and from work.

This factor directly relates to one of the most important areas of our life we are concerned with: Time. By having more time, this raises the overall quality of life for the entire family.

"Rick found us a home in a very fast market. Thank you for the excellent job!"
Eric & Viva Young

Appealing Neighborhood or Subdivision

Most buyers look for a home in a specific neighborhood or subdivision. Homes take less time to sell if they are in a sought-after neighborhood or subdivision.

Childcare

Buyers with children are looking for easy access to quality childcare. It is optimal for childcare to be located close to home because this is usually the first stop when leaving in the morning and last stop at the end of a busy work day.

Trees and Landscaping

Green is good! Homes that have trees appeal to more buyers. Some buyers prefer established neighborhoods with big trees and private backyards.

In our 68 years of combined real estate experience, we have never had a buyer say they want a home without trees. Trees and quality landscaping enhance the seller's property. One caution sellers must take into consideration is the size and location of the trees when planting.

Corner Lot

There are many negatives and positives to having a corner lot. If the property borders a busy street, this can be a negative. It creates twice as much sidewalk, more shoveling, more maintenance, and less backyard. There can also be a lack of privacy because you have a street in front of the home and another street on the side of the home. This can create more traffic noise.

Some positives of a corner lot are having a home on one side only. Sometimes corner lots are larger, making the backyard more accessible.

A corner lot also enables you to have your garage doors on the side of the house as opposed to being on the front of the home. A corner lot may also give you the opportunity to add a second garage. This can create better curb appeal to buyers.

Corner lots also allow a home to be built on a 45 degree angle to the street in order to add more privacy and have greater curb appeal.

Cul-de-sac Lots

Cul-de-sac lots also create several positive and negative points that influence certain buyers in different ways. With this type of lot, there is low traffic. However, there is limited parking and not many places to move snow in the winter months. Also, when traffic enters and leaves the cul-de-sac, the car headlights will shine across most homes in the cul-de-sac.

Cul-de-sac lots are sought-after because they are larger than average lots, which in turn create a very large, private backyard for family fun and entertaining. They also have less sidewalk with minimal front maintenance.

Most of the traffic in a cul-de-sac will only be from neighbors, which is a major benefit to buyers with children. We've seen children set up a baseball diamond or play street hockey because lack of traffic.

"Life is either a daring adventure or nothing."
Helen Keller

Low Traffic Streets

Buyers with children look for low traffic streets for the simple fact of safety and security. Buyers also directly associate low traffic streets with quieter neighborhoods.

Heavy traffic streets negatively affect the selling price, as it appeals to fewer buyers. A positive factor of high traffic streets is they will most likely be a snow route and are usually cleared first for safer travels. Some buyers like to live on a snow route.

Most bus routes run on through streets, making it easier for some buyers to get public transportation.

Least Expensive vs. Most Expensive

When discussing the least expensive house on the block vs. the most expensive house of the block, we have found it is best if your home's price point falls into the middle of a price range for an area. This is because if your home is at the top of the price range, you are going to pull up the homes on the bottom of the price range. Also, if you live in the most expensive home on the block, the other properties could pull your sales price down as well.

It is much more difficult for buyers to justify a higher price on your home if the homes in the area are at a lower price. The Messerschmidt Team will use our years of experience in negotiation to get you a higher price if your home falls in this category.

Most buyers typically search for homes and buy homes in an area where prices of the homes are similar.

As stated earlier, the location of the home is the most important factor to the buyer because buyers are purchasing a home based on their wants and needs for a location. As the wants and needs change for each buyer, so does the location of their perfect house. It is the job of the Messerschmidt Team to bring to you pre-qualified buyers whose wants and needs are in harmony with the traits and benefits of your home so it can be sold quickly and to the right buyer. *The more appealing the location to a buyer's needs, the faster your home is sold.*

"We want to thank you for everything. Everything was so organized.
Everything went so quickly! Thank you again!"
Olive/Harold Smith

Buyers Shop by Location

There truly is a buyer for every location and it is our job to make sure the right buyers are walking through your home in order to save you an enormous amount of time and money.

An example of this would be having a house that is right next to a factory. The employees of that factory may want to live close to work while other buyers have no desire to live next to the factory. Some people don't want to live close to work, while with others it is important to be close to their place of business.

"Most of the shadows of this life are caused by our standing in our own sunshine."
Ralph Waldo Emerson

Neighborhood Changes

Changes in your neighborhood can have negative or positive effect on the sale of your home. For example, a negative may be when a neighborhood gains a high number of rental properties. Neighborhoods that are primarily composed of rental properties instead of owner-occupied properties can change the entire look and feel of the neighborhood negatively. This factor can be out of your control.

Another neighborhood change can happen when the federal government changes the flood zone areas.

The appeal of an area can also change when major retail or commercial stores move into or out of your area, such as grocery stores, restaurants, and so forth.

The loss or addition of schools and changing school boundaries can also have a negative or a positive effect on the sale of your home.

"I've used several Realtors over the years, but Rick is the best!"
Jerre Brammeier

The buyer will pick or exclude a location because of the topics listed above.

Unfortunately, the sale and price of your home can be affected by your neighbor's home condition, such as color, maintenance, and curb appeal.

Buyers not only look at your house, but they also look at your neighbor's house and the surrounding homes. These all play an integral part in the buyer's decision to purchase your property.

Zoning Changes

There are federal, state, and city zoning changes that can affect the salability of your home. For example, a residential neighborhood can change from single family to multifamily zoning. Zoning changes occur around hospitals as they grow and expand.

There was a particular circumstance where a gentleman had a house close to a hospital and the block behind his property was rezoned. A parking lot was installed behind his house, which hurt the value of his home.

As our city expands, changes like widening streets are necessary. When the city annexes ground, a complete neighborhood could be brought into the city limits, and then an assessment for water and sewer would have to be levied on all property owners.

You may not have control over changes that will happen with zoning or conditioning of a subdivision, even though these changes can adversely affect the price of your home. It is our job as your REALTOR® to try to market your home to a particular buyer regardless of the changes that have happened in your area.

These are all examples of changes that are out of your control. One important thing you can control is the real estate team you choose to work with. It is our job to advise you on how these changes can affect the sale and price of your home.

*More on Condition: What Sellers Need to Consider

"The thing always happens that you really believe in,
and the belief in a thing makes it happen."
Frank Loyd Wright

As we have stated earlier—and it's worth repeating here—you only get one chance to make a first impression. The first impression literally sets the tone for how the buyers feel as they view the rest of the property. This fact cannot be stressed enough.

If the buyer walks into a neat and clean house, that is the perception and emotional tone they will carry with them throughout the viewing of your home. You only have about 30 seconds to get the buyer emotionally attached to your home, and once the emotional tone has been set, it remains with the buyer. Everything must be PERFECT! If the buyer has to overcome objections in the first minute of showing your property, the likelihood that you will get a good offer is drastically reduced.

Buyers don't typically want to do any work; they want their home move-in-ready. We advise sellers to look at their home objectively, through a buyer's eyes. After all, if the seller doesn't care enough to fix up their home, why should the buyer care enough to make an offer? This may sound a little direct, but these ideas sell homes and get results.

This is why so many "For Sale By Owners" completely and utterly fail. They cannot emotionally detach themselves from their home. They are not getting professional advice.

One of the secrets to selling your home is to make it look like you've never lived in it. This is a simple statement, but is very necessary if you want to get top dollar for your house.

Think of it this way: if you are going to sell your car, you will shampoo the carpets, clean the inside, steam clean the engine, take out the door dings, clean the wheels, possibly buy new mats for the floor—you get the idea. You set it aside and try not to drive it so it is always ready to be shown. The point we are trying to make is, top shape gives you top dollar.

We strongly recommend our clients clean their home every morning. Your home must be in top shape so the buyer does not find any negatives.

We help you to ensure that your home is staged correctly. Here is a list of questions you might have:

- Should I paint?
- Do I replace carpet or give allowance?
- Should I landscape?
- What about smoking and pets?
- What is depersonalization?
- How do I add "Sizzlemanship"?
- Do I need closet organizers and extra storage?
- Is my garage too full?
- Do I need a storage unit?
- What about traffic patterns?
- What is de-cluttering?
- Does my home need updating?

Should I Paint?

Buyers look for freshly painted homes. You need to have up-to-date colors. You can't have chipping or peeling paint inside or out.

Typically, more earth-toned or neutral colors appeal to a wider range of buyers because their furnishings and personal belongings work in a neutral setting.

Do I Replace Carpet or Give Allowance?

"Alone we can do so little; together we can do so much."
Helen Keller

In our experience, allowances do not work because lenders do not typically allow them. Also, buyers think it costs twice as much as it really does to replace carpet.

Buyers who read in marketing material, "seller to give carpeting allowance," perceive the house as being in bad condition. New carpet not only helps to sell your home, new carpet also helps you get more money for your home.

Should I Landscape?

The NAR says 94% of the buyers search for homes first on the internet. In other words, they make the decision to personally view your home solely based on curb appeal. This could consist of only a picture of the front of your home.

Landscaping is crucial to the sale of your home. Here are some things you can do to improve the appeal of your property:

- Remove dead bushes
- Trim overgrown shrubbery and grass
- Wash sidewalks
- Replace cracked entrance concrete
- Be sure driveway and sidewalks are in great condition

Don't forget about the front door:

- Front door area should be spotless—100% clean
- Freshly painted
- No cobwebs
- No torn carpet or rugs
- No negatives at all

What About Smoking and Pets?

Few things will destroy the sale of a home faster than smoke or pet odor. Bottom line, if you have pet smell or smoke smell in your house, you will be lucky to get an offer, and if you do, it will be very low.

We've had buyers take one step in the front door and if they smell either smoke or pet odors they turn right around and walk out. You need to do everything you can to make your home smell like it's never contained pets or smokers.

What is Depersonalization?

Depersonalization is neutralizing the home of personal pictures and effects. If there are too many of your personal items in the house, buyers cannot visualize it as their home. This is why model homes have neutral settings and accessories. We help you identify items that could potentially repel a buyer.

We also strongly recommend that all collectibles be boxed and stored. This will give the buyer the opportunity to see their items in the house. Although these may seem like minor details, these little things make a big difference in the sale of your home.

How Do I Add "Sizzlemanship"?

"Sizzlemanship" is adding the sparkle to your home. This is the art of having everything perfect, in top condition. These are just a few examples of how you can add "Sizzlemanship" to your home:

- ✓ Windows cleaned
- ✓ Carpet clean
- ✓ Furnace tops clean
- ✓ Water heater tops clean
- ✓ Storage room organized
- ✓ Shades up
- ✓ Toilet lids down
- ✓ Eliminate all pet odors and remove pets
- ✓ No smoking in the home

"Rick went above and beyond to make our purchase a pleasant experience. Rick definitely worked with us and for us. We highly recommend him and will hopefully have the opportunity to use Rick again in the future."
Gilbert & Gwen Sieg

If there is any way to have your pet out of the house or at a sitter's, we strongly recommend this step be taken. Be sure all remnants of pets are removed. This could include pet mats, bowls, and litter boxes.

If you can't remove your pet, you will need to kennel your animal in a lower level room or garage. We know and understand your pet is an integral part of your family, but pets can interfere with the showing process of your home. Some buyers may eliminate your home if your pet is running freely through the house.

Do I Need Closet Organizers and Extra Storage?

We strongly recommend making all your closets half-full. If all closets are full, the buyers will get the impression that there is not enough storage space.

Most closets benefit immensely by having custom shelving done by a professional. Spending money on closet organization is a good investment to add value to your home. Medium to upper end homes must have professionally installed custom closet organizers. It is important to understand that buyers absolutely look for this; it is a major factor to "Sizzlemanship" and is a WOW factor that stimulates emotional appeal.

For more information on closet consultation, design, and implementation, please refer to page 75.

"Thanks for all the help. Your professionalism and hard work are to be commended."
Greg Selle

Is My Garage Too Full?

Typically, most buyers are concerned with the size of the garage more than the things inside, but a cleaned and tidy garage helps your home sell. Boxes—as long as they're neatly stacked—are not typically a big issue.

Do I Need a Storage Unit?

Again, a house that is too full looks too small to the buyer. Your home needs to look spacious and open. If necessary, get a storage space to hold your extra belongings.

What are Traffic Patterns?

A traffic pattern is the flow of foot traffic through your home. We help to assure traffic areas are wide open and clear to give the buyer a feeling of having more than enough space. If buyers have to step around your furniture and/or decorative personal items, they usually get the perception that the house is too small for them.

When we are showing homes, there will normally be three to five people on average walking together through your home. With this many people in one group, cluttered traffic patterns give the feel that the home is too small.

What is De-Cluttering?

This step involves removing unnecessary items that are taking up too much space. Sellers need to have all surfaces cleared, including kitchen and bath countertops as well as all shelving. The more furniture you have, the more cluttered the space will appear. When you de-clutter the room of access furniture, it appears larger.

Does My Home Need Updating?

There are two types of updating: one is updating to add pleasure and enjoyment to your home, such as adding a theater room or a swimming pool, and the other is improving your homes sale-ability. We are talking about the second.

The secret is to make your home look like a million dollars without spending it. We will walk you through your home, room by room and give you advice on how to get top dollar.

4. Financing Terms

"If you don't know where you are going, you'll end up someplace else."
Yogi Berra

A major factor to a successful sale is our ability and willingness to work with other professionals who will do the absolute best job for you. This is why we have selected Brian Spaan from First Bank & Trust to write a chapter about finances and handle some common mortgage questions we are asked on a regular basis. Brian is a professional mortgage lender and one of the best in this area; we strongly recommend you refer to his chapter towards the back of this book or contact him for any mortgage related questions.

5. REALTOR®

The Messerschmidt Team Mission Statement

Dedicated to Providing Total Client Satisfaction through the Highest Quality of Ethical and Professional Real Estate Services.

There are tremendous benefits to working with a full service real estate team like The Messerschmidt Team. Imagine playing a game of basketball that was four people against one. Who do you think would win? Of course the team with four players would easily defeat the team of only one. This analogy is a perfect demonstration of the power of working with a full service real estate team as opposed to only one agent.

With The Messerschmidt Team, you get three full time real estate brokers with one common goal—to sell your home. The fourth member of our team is a client services manager with over a decade of experience. This gives you instant access to a real person absolutely anytime between the hours of 8 A.M. to 5 P.M. every workday. No more leaving voicemails and waiting for responses. With our team, there will always be someone available to help you.

No one person can be in two places at once. There will be many opportunities missed if you are only working with one REALTOR®. An agent who spends all their time in the office has no time to show and sell your home. Our client services manager frees up our time so we can do just that. This puts us ahead of our competition because: *if you don't have an assistant you are one.*

Who's Selling Your Home When Your REALTOR® Goes on Vacation?

Our team not only brings more working hours to the sale of your home, but we also bring more selling ideas, more experience, and more options for you.

We have four main objectives when we list your home for sale:

1. To get as many qualified buyers as possible into your home until it is sold.
2. To communicate the results of our activities bi-weekly to you.
3. To assist you in getting the highest possible dollar value for your property with the least amount of problems.
4. To constantly look for the best possible methods of exposing your property to the potential buyers in the market.

When you are working with our full service team, you have four professionals with a single goal in mind: to meet all of the outlined objectives and sell your home.

"Thanks for everything and making things go so smoothly with such a short close time!"
Karla & Dale Derynck

Here are a few of the designations The Messerschmidt Team has earned:

- Certified Residential Specialist (CRS): This designation is held by elite REALTORS® and is only achieved by the top 5% in the U.S. real estate industry. This certification is a symbol of sales experience and educational development. A very high level of education is required as well as documented records of past listing and selling properties.
- Graduate REALTOR® Institute (GRI): This represents a REALTOR® who has made a commitment to provide a high level of service to their clients. GRI certified REALTORS® are highly trained in many areas of real estate, as 90 hours of coursework are required to receive this designation.
- Accredited Buyer's Representative (ABR): This designation specifically trains a REALTOR® in representing the real estate buyer. A REALTOR® must complete a comprehensive, two-day REBAC course of intensive training on buyer representation. They must also complete a definite amount of real estate transactions in which they work solely as the buyer representative.
- Certified New Home Specialist (CNHS): This is recognized as real estate's top certification for training and professionalism in working with builders and new home purchases. A CNHS agent has proven his or her ability to work effectively with consumers and builders to assure everyone benefits from each real estate transaction.
- Residential Construction Certified (RCC): A RCC designee has been tested and proven a thorough understanding of the terminology, methods, and processes of residential construction.

SELLING PROCESS

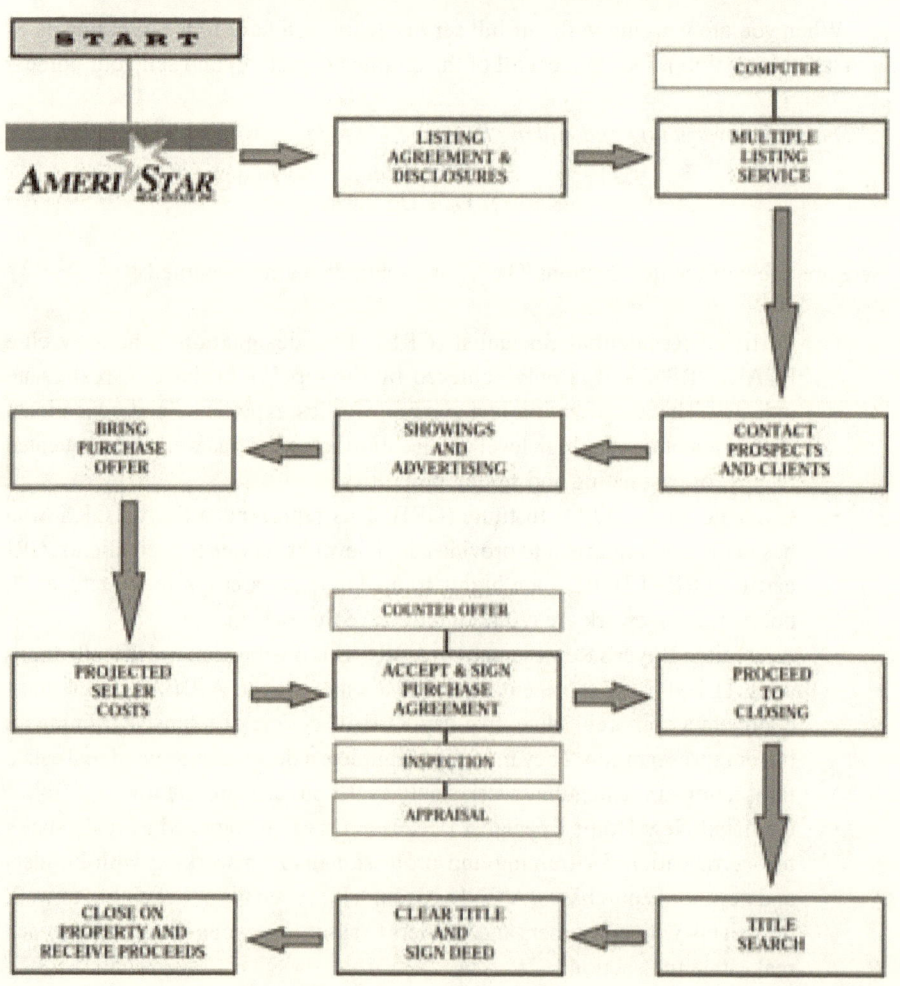

START

AMERI STAR
REAL ESTATE, INC.

LISTING
AGREEMENT &
DISCLOSURES

COMPUTER

MULTIPLE
LISTING
SERVICE

CONTACT
PROSPECTS
AND CLIENTS

SHOWINGS
AND
ADVERTISING

BRING
PURCHASE
OFFER

PROJECTED
SELLER
COSTS

COUNTER OFFER

ACCEPT & SIGN
PURCHASE
AGREEMENT

INSPECTION

APPRAISAL

PROCEED
TO
CLOSING

TITLE
SEARCH

CLEAR TITLE
AND
SIGN DEED

CLOSE ON
PROPERTY AND
RECEIVE PROCEEDS

BUYING PROCESS

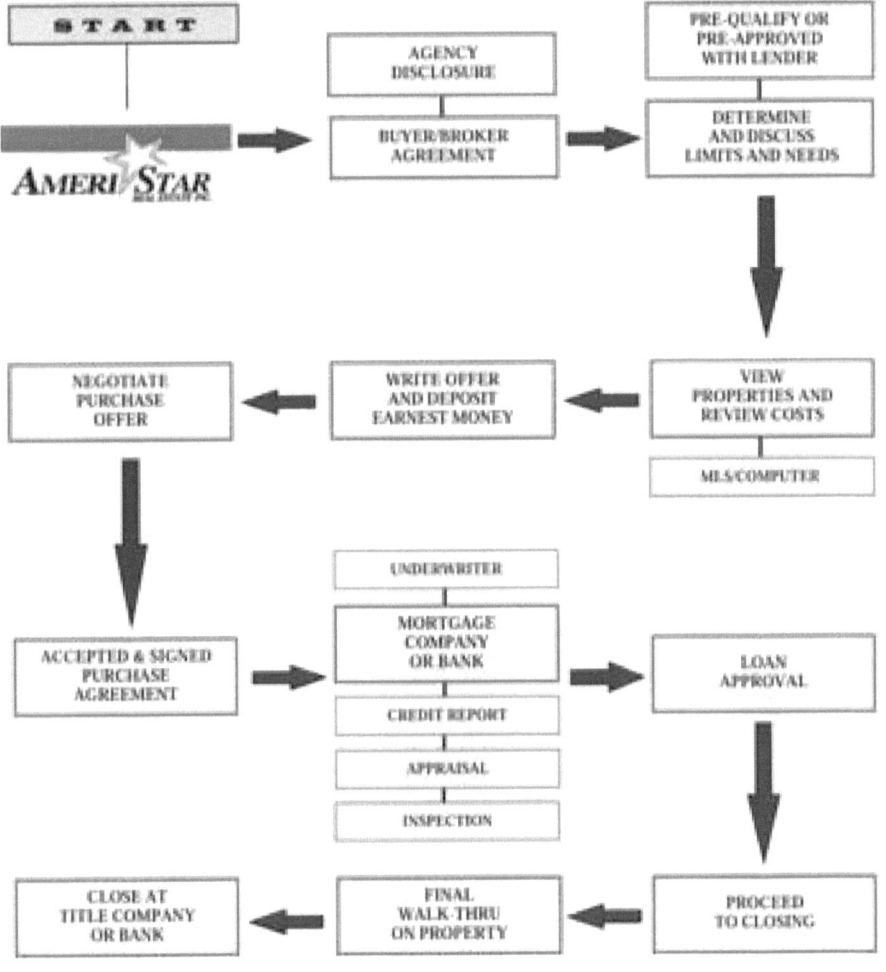

For Buyers

Why Should You Work with a REALTOR® with Designations?

More designations means more education, and more education means more knowledge. This will assure you a smoother transaction to help you fulfill your real estate needs.

We believe strongly in advancing education, as evidenced by our list of designations on page 36. If we are not growing, we are dying, and a major factor of our long-term success has been our commitment to education.

A real estate agent is a REALTOR® when he or she becomes a member of the NATIONAL ASSOIATION OF REALTORS®, *The Voice for Real Estate®,* the world's largest professional association. The term "REALTOR®" is a registered collective membership mark that identifies a real estate professional who is a member of the NATIONAL ASSOCIATION OF REALTORS® and abides by its strict Code of Ethics.

REALTORS® are bound by a code of ethics written by assisting appropriate regulatory bodies to eliminate practices which may damage the public or which might discredit or bring dishonor to the real estate profession.

> *"The most important single ingredient in the formula of success*
> *is knowing how to get along with people."*
> Theodore Roosevelt

The Extra Mile

It's not only our job to sell your home to all potential buyers, but also to sell your home to all REALTORS® throughout the Multiple Listing Service. The Messerschmidt Team will absolutely go the extra mile when working with other REALTORS® on the showing and selling of your home. We've actually helped agents from other companies to write offers on our listings when their broker was unavailable.

We look at each transaction from all angels to make sure it goes smoothly to the close.

Working with Other Professionals
"A leader is a dealer in hope."
Napoleon Bonaparte

We have worked extremely hard to build a reputation of honesty and trustworthiness not only to sellers and buyers, but also to other REALTORS® and professionals.

The Messerschmidt Home Selling System makes it easy for other REALTORS® to work with us in the sale of our listings. We value the relationships we have with other REALTORS® and respect all the work they do with us and for the Sioux Falls Community.

Where Do Our Buyers Come From?

A powerful statistic with our team is the fact that **84%** of our business comes from past clients and their friends, **10%** of our business comes from open houses, and **6%** comes from all other sources.

Think of a fisherman for a moment. No matter how big the boat or how effective the tackle, if he or she only has one line in the water at a time, the odds this person will catch any fish are highly unlikely. The same idea applies to the sale of your home. We use multiple lines in the water. We utilize unique and cutting edge strategies to capture the buyer and sell them your home.Buyers come from many different sources and trying to get buyers to look at a specific home takes many years of experience and knowledge. We track buyers, so we know exactly where our buyers are coming from.

As stated earlier, keep in mind we are fulltime REALTORS®. When we wake up in the morning, we are thinking about how to sell your property. A For Sale By Owner may work only a couple hours a week to sell their house, and that is one reason why the FSBO failure rate is extremely high. We are working 24/7 to sell our listings.

You might ask, *"How can you work 24/7?"* Here are a few of the ways we do that:

- Multiple Listing Service
  This is where we can market your home to all other REALTORS® 24/7.

- Web Sites
  We use multiple websites to market your home.

- Advertising
  Remember, we expose your home through many different media such as print, TV, and radio.

39

- Open Houses

  We know open houses are the best way to get the public through your home. Buyers love open houses. Buyers find your home on our websites and then come to our open houses. All the systems we use to sell your home are driven to entice buyers to come view your home. Remember, buyers won't purchase your home until they get inside and view it.

- Pictures

  A picture is worth a thousand words. We take high quality digital photos that will appeal to a buyer and entice them into viewing the property.

"Steve has been in the business so long that I just associate the Messerschmidt name with the realty business. He's very professional, very friendly, always has a smile and is so efficient. Everything was explained to us in everyday person's language. Also I really appreciated the pictures and handsome advertisement of our home. He made it so easy! Thank you, Steve!"
Deb Goldstine

The Messerschmidt Team Provides Full Service Real Estate

The aforementioned list contains just a few of our 179 typical actions, research steps, procedures, processes, and review stages in a successful residential real estate transaction. Depending on the transaction, some may take minutes, hours, or even days to complete. More importantly, they reflect the level of skill, knowledge, and attention to detail required in today's real estate transaction and further underscore the importance of having help and guidance from someone who fully understands the process.

Never forget that we have pledged to uphold the stringent, enforceable tenets of the REALTOR® Code of Ethics in our professional dealings with the public. Not every real estate licensee holds REALTOR® membership. We do! Call us today to get started with The Messerschmidt Team Selling System.

"Working with The Messerschmidt Team was terrific in helping us purchase our own and selling our existing home. The response time to our questions was beyond our expectations. Thank you for your service, we will definitely recommend you to our friends and family."
Rita Patzwald

Questions You Must Ask Before Choosing Your REALTOR®

In order to assist you in making the correct decision as to which real estate team will be most effective for the sale of your home, we have assembled a list of the most important questions to ask a prospective REALTOR®:

"How long have you been in business?"
- This will clearly show you the level of knowledge the realtor possesses. Experience matters, and is always the most important factor. The Messerschmitt Team has over 68 years of combined experience in real estate.

"How many homes have you sold?"
- This question answers how active the prospective REALTOR® is. You must discover exactly how successful they really are at selling homes. Results don't lie. We have sold over 2,900 homes in our combined experience.

"How many homes have you sold in my area?"
- This displays how knowledgeable the realtor is in your neighborhood and price range. Some agents can only work effectively in certain price ranges and in certain neighborhoods. We sell homes in all price ranges and neighborhoods due to our vast experience.

"Do you have an assistant?"
- As we've mentioned, the truth is that if the REALTOR® doesn't have an assistant, that REALTOR® *is* the assistant. The main job of a REALTOR® is to work with buyers and sellers and to be out selling homes. No REALTOR® can effectively sell homes by sitting in the office. It is just that simple. A real estate transaction takes a tremendous amount of paperwork, follow up, and in-office time, and we have carefully hand selected a professional assistant who has been working with our team for over 12 years.

"Are you a full time agent?"

- Would you go to a part time doctor to seek medical advice? Of course not. You see the point we are making here. As full time agents, we are finding ways to sell your home each and every day. If your REALTOR® is part time they are hoping someone else will sell your home for them. In today's real estate world, buyers expect information on homes almost immediately, not when a part time REALTOR® gets done with their first job. We don't mean to sound harsh, but it is absolutely crucial to understand this. Working with a full time agent could mean a difference of thousands of dollars in your pocket.

"Are you part of a real estate team?"

- With a team, there is always someone available to give information or show your home at any given time. Most REALTORS® don't list one single property. They list multiple properties and must divide their time between them. When listing with The Messerschmidt Team, a major benefit to the seller is that someone is always working on the sale of your home. One REALTOR® cannot be in more than one place at a time.

"What designations/additional education do you have?"

- This shows whether a REALTOR® is willing to invest in themselves and pursue more knowledge. We have numerous designations (listed on page 36). By increasing our knowledge, this allows us to continually get new ideas and stay on the cutting edge of marketing your home. The real estate market is ever-changing. If your REALTOR® is not constantly educating him or herself, he or she will not be as effective. We are always looking for and implementing innovative ideas, techniques, and systems that help our sellers get their homes sold.

"Do you have a large inventory of homes?"

- Some realtors are listing agents—not selling agents—which means they do nothing but list as many homes as possible, but never plan on selling any of those homes.
- Our clients and their friends keep coming back to us because we sell homes. We are not there to just list the home, we are there to get your home sold for you.

"How many days does it take to get a home sold through the Multiple Listing Service?"

- This information gives you a benchmark on how active the market is in your home's price range. It is important to know this information so you can set up your timetable and organize your future plans.

"How many days does it take you to sell a home?"

• This will determine if the REALTOR® is selling homes faster than the average sales time on the Multiple Listing Service. If the REALTOR'S® average sale time takes longer than the average MLS time, this clearly indicates the REALTOR'S® lack of experience and lack of marketing skills.

"What is the MLS list price to sales price?"

• This is the difference between the list price (the price the seller asked for their home) and the sales price (what the buyer was willing to pay).

"What is your list price to sale price?"

• This question will help you identify if the REALTOR® is overpricing their listings. This is called buying a listing, which is when a REALTOR® overprices your home only for the purpose of getting the listing. This also shows if that REALTOR® understands the market and pricing, and how effective at negotiating the REALTOR® will be for you. This is one of our greatest strengths—negotiating on your behalf.

"What are you going to do to get my house sold?"

✓ What is your marketing plan?
✓ Do you advertise?
✓ Do you use the Internet?
✓ Do you have your own website?
✓ What other websites are you on?
✓ Do you run open houses?

There are realtors out there who use the "3 P Promotion":

1. **Put** the home on MLS
2. **Put** a sign in the front yard
3. **Pray** someone else (like the Messerschmidt Team) sells it

There is no question that the number one mistake sellers make when choosing a REALTOR® is selecting one who tells them the highest list price for their home. We have seen sellers choose the realtor who tells them the highest price or the price the seller really wants to hear. Then, unfortunately, the home sits on the market for so long that it becomes market worn and everyone is wondering, *"What is wrong with that home?"*

When the seller decides to sell their home, they have two decisions to make. The first decision is selecting the realtor who is going to do the best job at selling the home to the public and to other realtors. Then the second decision is setting the correct price for the home.

We will always tell you the truth about your home. We will always tell you what you need to hear and not necessarily what you always want to hear.

"Loyal was very helpful! This was my first sale—lived in home 24 years. Neighborhood 45 years. It was HOME for me and my husband and son. We had no idea of what we should do to sell or buy so he was our guide in everything that needed to be done. Thank you very much Loyal."
Vernon and Michele Dandurand

Three Income Earning Strategies

There are three basic income-earning strategies that are taught throughout the world. We strongly recommend not only putting yourself into favorable employment but also putting your money into employment as well.

The more you understand how money works, the more you will learn to value your money. As you value money, you begin to save it and eventually invest it. Below is a brief outline of the three basic ways for you to earn money. As you increase your financial knowledge you will eventually increase your financial power.

Strategy One

The first strategy to earn money is to simply trade you time for money. In this strategy, you will be working for an hourly wage or salary. Well over 90% of the population works in this strategy, and they earn less than 10% of all the money that is being earned. These statistics appear to be out of balance, but they are true.

When you initially think of working for an hourly wage or salary, you may think of white or blue collar employees for large corporations. However, lawyers work in this strategy, as well as doctors. Almost everyone is trading their time for money.

There is a very large problem with this strategy and it is called saturation. If you want to earn more money, you must put in more hours. You will eventually run out of time and hours to work because, unfortunately, we only have so much time.

When you work in this strategy, you are trading your life for money. Time is one of the most important things we have, and once it is spent, we never get it back.

> *"Time is more valuable than money. You can get more money,*
> *but you cannot get more time."*
> Jim Rohn

Now, even though we have mostly pointed out the negatives for this strategy, there are a few good aspects as well. One of the major benefits is you will have the security of always getting a check on a certain date. Just because you are in a large corporation, however, doesn't mean you are secure. Remember, you will never find true security in anything outside of yourself. If you don't have it inside, you don't have it.

As you set your financial goals, if you want true wealth you must continue to read on through the next two strategies.

Strategy Two

Strategy number two is earning money by investing. You could say this is trading money to earn money.

This can be a very good strategy if you have the money to invest. A very small percentage of the population follows this strategy simply because most people may not have the financial capabilities or education to operate in this strategy.

In order to work in this strategy, a tremendous amount of knowledge regarding finances and investments will be required. If you lack expertise or experience when it comes to investment strategies, you will want to seek the counsel of an experienced professional. Find someone who is willing and able to counsel or mentor you.

This strategy brings us to the most powerful way to leverage the income you have earned and have your money working for you 24/7, which is Strategy Three.

Strategy Three

The third strategy is the best way to earn money. Approximately 1% of the population works in this strategy, and they earn more than 90% of all the money that is being earned. Much like the first strategy, these numbers can appear to be out of balance, but they are true.

In this strategy you earn your money through multiple sources of income. You can go all throughout history as far back as the ancient Babylonians and you will discover the wealthiest people earn their money through multiple sources. They have learned to leverage their time through the efforts of other people or systems.

Leverage is one of the most important words when it comes to money. When you do it properly, you can accomplish larger goals in less time.

Here is an example that will illustrate the power of leverage. Try to imagine lifting a 1,500 pound rock with your own strength. There is no one who could do this. If you were to use the proper leverage, however, you could lift that boulder with very little strain.

Could you lift a full sized car with one arm? No. But think about the Washington Pavilion for a moment. Have you seen the display on the east side of the building? If you have, you know you can lift a full size car with one arm very easily. In fact, you have probably witnessed small children lifting the car. How can this be true?

REAL ESTATE FOR THE GENERATIONS

The kids are able to lift the car by tugging a long rope that is attached to a large levee system. Several feet away, there is a full size car on the opposite end of the levee system that will go up and down as the children tug the rope.

This is a perfect demonstration of how the proper leverage can enable you to accomplish goals that seem impossible to do with your strength alone.

Leverage can be applied in many different ways. The concept of leverage works very effectively in the previous example, and it will work equally as well with money. A financial goal that would be almost impossible for you to reach in your current circumstances will be achieved relatively easily with the proper use of leverage.

Through investing in real estate, you can enter in this third income earning strategy and begin leveraging the wonderful asset of real estate properties to increase your personal wealth.

Although investing in real estate is a tremendously long-term strategy, we strongly recommend you seek the advice of a highly experience real estate team, like The Messerschmidt Team. As with any large investment, this is something that should be thought through from many different angles as well as analyzed thoroughly to maximize your investment as much as possible.

> *"The art is not in making money, but in keeping it."*
> Proverb

Does Real Estate Investing Fit Into My Financial Plan?

It is essential to make sure your potential real estate investment fits into your overall financial plan before you make any buying decisions. Ask yourself these questions to make sure you are ready:

1. Do I have retirement savings?
2. Do I have other investments?
3. Is liquidity a problem for me?
4. Do I have a large amount of unpredictable cash flow?
5. Do I need tax advantages that a sound real estate investment could provide me?
6. Do I want this property to provide me with retirement income?
7. Do I see this investment as long term or do I want immediate income?

Answering these questions will give you a good idea if you are ready for a real estate investment and if an investment of this type fits into your financial plan. We will go over these questions with you in our initial meeting to help you make the right choice for your financial goals.

Tips for Better Investing

Here are some tips to keep in the forefront of your mind when you are investing in real estate:

- The focus should be cash on cash
- Make your money on the buy
- Pay good wages to retain good talent when it comes to renovations
- Do not determine your return based on the price of the property, but on the return you will receive from the equity you have in the property.
- Avoid unique homes
- Always get pre-approved for your loan
- See the potential of the unit as opposed to the condition it is in today
- Stick with smaller units and don't go overboard on renovations
- Be sure to keep in mind that the asking price is not the final price
- Don't expect short-term appreciation to save you
- Don't worry entirely about the cap rate
- Make sure your assets are properly protected from lawsuits
- Have a trusted list of repair professionals to get your unit market ready quickly after a tenant moves out
- Never overlook deductions
- Don't follow the temptation to buy more properties than you can successfully manage
- Buy in the best possible location while staying within your budget
- Consider purchasing a building for your brokerage office

Five Tips on How to Gain Income through Real Estate Investments

When you invest in stock certificates, your primary source of income is money earned from the appreciation of the stock value. When investing in bonds, your source of income is income yield on the interest that has been paid by the bonds. With a real estate investment, however, there are many more ways available to you to earn a significant return on investment. Here are only five of the many ways that your real estate investment can not only appreciate in value, but simultaneously provide you with positive cash flow.

1. Inflation is Good

Even though a fixed mortgage will remain constant, inflation will increase construction costs as well as the number of renters. An increase in population will increase housing demands, which will also drive rent prices higher if the supply cannot keep up with the demand.

2. Higher Value Due to Appreciation

Real estate has historically proven to be a great source of income through the appreciation of investment properties. Even though the market is never 100% predictable, Sioux Falls has remained a great market for investors.

3. Rental Income Cash Flow

An intelligently selected and properly managed rental unit will be an excellent source of income through the rental payments. When you invest in real estate, as opposed to other investment alternatives, you have a slightly higher control over the risks associated with the property and the cash flow.

4. Enhancing Your Investment

As your property is producing positive cash flow, you can choose to enhance the property. That will increase the resale value when you decide to liquidate the property as an investment.

5. Hit a Home Run

A "Home Run" occurs when you have a unique opportunity to purchase below market value and sell for significantly higher in the short-term future. Although people are typically motivated by the home run investment initially, we don't recommend you bank on this happening, even though it is possible. Should you be so fortunate as to work with a highly experienced real estate team and locate a great property, this could be a quick way to increase your overall net worth and your investment portfolio.

The Messerschmidt Team has the experience and the knowledge you need in order to quickly locate value priced properties and guide you into making the right decision for you and your financial goals.

"Very professional. Keeps current with changes in financing. Knows the market."
David Park

Getty-Midwest
Est. 1899

Mike L. Wilds—President
Getty Abstract & Title Company
5800 S. Remington Pl., Ste 120
Sioux Falls, SD 57108
www.gettyabstract.com
Phone: (605) 336-0490

At Getty Abstract & Title Company, our goal and focus is to deliver consistently high quality customer service. It is the mission of every employee and officer of Getty to do whatever is possible to satisfy the needs of our clients in a professional and timely manner. The culture of quality customer driven service has enabled Getty to succeed and grow over its hundred and ten years in business.

Nothing in business or commerce is static and that is particularly true in real estate. Getty Abstract & Title Company has evolved to meet the requirements of the market and the changing needs of our customers. What started in 1899 as an abstract company transcribing and reporting the history and status of real property for local attorneys, real estate agents, and lenders has evolved into a title insurance agency issuing title insurance policies on behalf of its underwriters that guarantee all forms of interest in real estate for investors across the country and around the globe; into an escrow closing company that handles all facets of real estate transfer and construction loan disbursement; and into a 1031 tax deferred exchange intermediary and accommodator. If any company stops improving the level of service they deliver to their customers, that company will not succeed long term. It is this philosophy and attitude that keeps everyone at Getty Abstract & Title Company progressive and consistently moving forward into its second century of operation.

Throughout this chapter, I want to give you not only an overview of the title process, but also answer some common questions we hear in our offices. Do not hesitate to contact our offices if you need further assistance.

What is Title Insurance?

Title insurance is an exclusively American invention. Its purpose was well stated in the first advertisement for title insurance back in the late 1800s:

"This company insures the purchase's of real estate and mortgages against loss from defective titles, liens, and encumbrances. Through these facilities [the] transfer of real estate and real estate securities can be made more speedily and with greater security than heretobefore." [circa 1876]

Protecting purchasers against loss is accomplished by the issuance of a title insurance policy, which states that if the status of the title to a parcel of real property is other than as represented, and if the insured suffers a loss as a result of title defect, the insurer will reimburse the insured for that loss and any related legal expenses up to the face amount of the policy.

Title insurance differs significantly from other forms of insurance. While the functions of most other forms of insurance is risk assumption through the pooling of risks for losses arising out of unforeseen future events (such as death or accidents), the primary purpose of title insurance is to eliminate risks and prevent losses caused by defects in title arising out of events that have happened in the past. To achieve this goal, title insurers perform an extensive search of the public records to determine whether there are any adverse claims or encumbrances that affect the subject real estate. Those claims or encumbrances are reported to the proposed insured and are either eliminated prior to the issuance of a title policy or, if acceptable to the proposed insured, their existence is excepted from coverage.

The Benefits of Title Insurance

Title insurance provides a broad range of benefits to the parties involved in a real estate transaction.

To the Purchaser of Real Estate...

The purchaser of real estate needs protection against serious financial loss due to a defect in the title to the property purchased. For a single, one-time premium, which is a modest amount in relationship to the value of the property, a buyer can receive the protection of a title insurance policy—a policy that is backed by the reserves and solvency of the issuing title insurance company. A title insurance policy will cover both claims arising out of title problems that could have been discovered in the public records, and those so-called "non-record" defects that could not be discovered in the record, even with the most complete search.

A title insurance policy will not only protect the insured owner, but also that person's heirs for as long as they hold title to the property, and even after they sell by warranty deed. The insuring company will not only satisfy any valid claim made against the insured's title, but it will pay for the costs and legal expenses of defending against a title claim.

To the Lender . . .

The overwhelming majority of mortgage loans made in the United States are made by persons who are acting in a fiduciary capacity—by savings and loan associations, savings banks, and commercial banks on behalf of their depositors, and by life insurance companies on behalf of their policyholders. Because they are lending other people's money (other people's savings or policyholders' funds) these lenders must be concerned with the safety of their mortgage investments.

A policy of title insurance provides a mortgage lender with a high degree of safety against the loss of security as a result of a title problem. This protection remains in effect for as long as the mortgage remains unsatisfied.

Title insurance companies also provide lenders with in-depth expertise on a wide variety of title related matters to facilitate the mortgage loan process, and to resolve differences among the various parties in the transaction.

To the Seller . . .

An owner of real property whose interest is insured by an owner's title insurance policy has the assurance that the title will be marketable, except for their own actions during the time of their ownership, when the property is sold. The title insurance policy protects the seller from financial damage if the seller's title is rejected by a prospective purchaser. Also, when the seller conveys with "warranties," which is traditional, the seller is protected if the buyer sues because of a breach of those warranties due to covered matters of which the seller had no knowledge.

To the Real Estate Attorney . . .

Title insurance enables the real estate attorney to provide the client with substantially greater protection than would be afforded by the attorney's opinion alone. The attorney's opinion is limited to recorded matters, may be time limited, and the client can only recover from the attorney if the attorney is found to be negligent.

To the Real Estate Broker . . .

The title insurance company and the real estate agent both seek to ensure that as many purchases as possible are closed to the satisfaction of all the principals in the transaction. From the broker's standpoint, the efficient and safe transfer of the title will result in client satisfaction, increased prestige, and continued business.

Apart from the security that title insurance offers, most brokers have experienced numerous instances in which title insurance personnel have enabled them to close transactions that otherwise would have been delayed. By helping to avoid delays the title insurer is able to facilitate the job of the real estate broker and to minimize the inconveniences and costs to the homebuyer.

To the Home Builder . . .

By providing various title insurance services and information to the home builder, the title insurance industry can and does assist the builder in identifying and evaluating building and use restrictions, easements, etc., in removing title problems that may arise, and in facilitating prompt and needed disbursement of construction funds from the construction lender. All of these services ultimately rebound to the benefit of the buyers of newly constructed homes.

To the Community In General . . .

Apart from the unique benefits title insurance offers to particular parties interested in a real estate transaction, title insurance companies can and do offer considerable assistance to public officials through their "title plants"—data banks of reorganized and indexed public records maintained by a title insurance company that can be used to verify the accuracy of the public record and to replace the public record in the event of loss or damage.

Much of the information contained in title plants is not readily available from other sources. This fund of information about the date of recent sales, representative sale prices, ownerships, area maps, use restrictions, surrounding properties, and a host of other matters pertinent to proposed projects, has helped representatives from all levels of government save countless hours and taxpayer dollars. In addition, title companies frequently help recording officers correct errors they discover in public indices and records.

Historical Developments

The need for title insurance arose historically from the fact that traditional methods of conveying real property did not provide adequate safety to the parties involved. Until a century ago, transferring title to real property was handled primarily by conveyancers who were responsible for all aspects of the transaction. The conveyancer conducted a title search to determine the ownership rights of the seller and any other rights, interests, liens, or encumbrances that might exist with respect to the property, and, based on its search, provide a signed abstract (or description) of the status of the title. Although the conveyancer was generally not a lawyer, that individual was recognized as an authority on real estate law. The origin of title insurance is directly traceable to the limited protection that the work of such a conveyancer provided to the purchaser of real property.

In 1868, the celebrated case of Watson v. Muirhead (57 Pa. 161) was filed in Pennsylvania. In that case, Muirhead, a conveyancer, had searched and provided a written report "abstract of title" for Watson, the purchaser of a parcel of real property. In good faith and after consulting an attorney, Muirhead chose to ignore certain recorded judgments and to report the title as good and unencumbered. On the basis of Muirhead's abstract, Watson went ahead with the purchase, but was subsequently presented with, and required to satisfy, the liens that Muirhead had concluded were not impairments to title. Watson sued Muirhead to recover his losses, but the Pennsylvania Supreme Court ruled that there was not negligence on the conveyancer's part and dismissed the case. Watson, an innocent purchaser who had suffered financial damages because of the encumbrances on his title, had no recourse.

The decision of Watson v. Muirhead demonstrated clearly that the existing conveyancing system could not provide total assurance to purchasers of real property that they would be safe and secure in their ownership. As a result of that decision, the Pennsylvania legislature shortly thereafter passed an act "to provide for the incorporation and regulation of title insurance companies." The first title company was founded in Philadelphia in 1876.

This new type of insurance (called "title insurance") addressed the concerns raised in Watson v. Muirhead by providing: (1) responsibility without proof of negligence, (2) financial protection through a reduction of the risk of insolvency, and (3) the assumption of risks beyond those disclosed in the public records (for which the conveyancer/abstractor was not liable).

Since the late 1800s, the title insurance industry has grown to where it now is an essential component in an overwhelming majority of real estate transactions in this country. The services provided by the title insurers may vary somewhat from one area of the country to another, reflecting the different laws, customs, and procedures of the various states and counties throughout the nation, but the essential purpose of these services is the same—to assist all of the parties in real estate transactions by ensuring that the acquisition or transfer of an interest in real estate can be effected with a maximum degree of efficiency, security, and safety.

Title Issues

The job of searching the public records to identify existing rights and interests is not an easy task. In many areas, the title to a property must be traced back to its source, which might be a royal grant, charter, or, in South Dakota, the United States government. The title searcher or abstracter reviews the public records to find all aspects of title that can be seen and recognized. From the title search, the title examiner produces an opinion of title, from which the Company will issue its insurance.

There are few titles—if any—that have a perfect history from their source, or root, to the present day. Each transfer of ownership is a "link" in what is referred to as the "chain of title." As each transaction or link takes place, there is potential for a problem. Even if the entire chain of title appears to be in order, the chain is still subject to interpretation. When searching a title, what we are trying to determine are the various rights and interests that make up each link in the chain as it has passed from one owner to another.

A "title" is composed of three basic elements.

1. Rights and interests that are disclosed in the public records or by physical inspection of the property, i.e. deeds, mortgages, leases, etc., parties in possession, utility easements, etc.
2. Rights and interests that are not recorded but exist, i.e. limitations imposed by laws and statutes, etc.
3. Rights and interests that are hidden, i.e. forgeries, secret marriages, and unknown heirs.

Every title is made up of many different "rights" and "interests" that may be owned by different people. The "owners" of the property own the most valuable of the property's rights and interests, but other people may also have rights to the property, such as easements for utilities or mortgages, etc.

Each title can be compared to sticks in a bundle. The rights and interests are represented by the sticks. The "owners" own what we call a "fee simple" title, that is, they have purchased the most vital and valuable sticks, including rights of possession, use, occupancy, enjoyment, inheritance, etc. Also, within the bundle are sticks that may be owned by other parties. These are called encumbrances, and may consist of easements, mortgages, liens, etc.

When a person purchases a parcel of real estate, it is not only the physical property itself that he or she acquires, but also the sellers' rights and interests, "the seller's title," in the property. It is essential for the prospective purchaser to know before the transaction takes place precisely what rights or interests the seller can convey. The purchaser also needs to know who else may have rights or interest in the property, and about any encumbrances against the property that may affect the use or enjoyment of the land. The title search must cover all these rights and interests.

Parties in a Transaction

There are few business transactions with more importance than those related to the sale and purchase of real estate. The purchase of a home is usually the largest, single expenditure most families will ever make. To these families, we at Getty Abstract & Title Company play a critical role in the real estate transaction.

In most cases, a property owner will approach a real estate agent and offer a property for sale. The agent will then advertise the property and conduct a search for potential buyers. Generally, a number of potential buyers will respond to the agent's listing, depending upon real estate market conditions and general economic conditions at the time. The agent, working with the client, then determines which of the potential buyers is financially qualified to enter into sale price negotiations with the property owner.

Once a qualified buyer is found and a sale of property is arranged for and completed, the agent is compensated in the form of a commission. This commission is normally paid by the property seller and is based on a percentage of the final sale price of the property. The actual dollar amount of the commission, as well as the general terms of the agent's services, are specified in a **listing contract** or **listing agreement**.

Once the buyer and seller have agreed on a purchase price, they enter into a Purchase Agreement or Contract. The contract sets out the terms of the agreement such as price, closing date, contingencies, etc. In some instances, the advice of a lawyer is sought by one or more of the parties to advise them on their rights or obligations under the Purchase Agreement, a legally binding contract that, once executed, defines and controls the sale and conveyance.

Most people do not have enough cash to purchase property on an all-cash basis and must therefore look toward one of the many sources of financing available today. The basic arrangement is that someone will lend the buyer enough money to purchase the property under certain conditions. The conditions require the purchaser to repay the monies according to a known repayment schedule, and pledge the property as security for the debt.

When you borrow money, the lender is in fact making an investment in which the lender will earn interest. Your payments will usually be made on a monthly basis and are calculated so that the entire amount of principal and interest due is repaid in a fixed number of years. If the entire debt will not be paid in this time (i.e., fully "amortized") the total amount left to be paid is called a "balloon" payment.

The lender first processes and underwrites the buyer's application. This involves ordering credit reports, appraisals, verification of salary, verification of debts, and possible investor and private mortgage insurance company approval. When loan approval appears likely, **title insurance** is ordered, commonly by the lender but often by the real estate agent.

Common Questions

As I stated at the beginning of the chapter, we are dedicated to giving you the highest level of service in the shortest time frame possible. One aspect to delivering quality service is by answering any questions our customers have. For this reason, I have gathered and arranged some frequently asked questions.

Please feel free to call our office to gain further information or to learn how we can make this process as easy and timely as possible.

What items are needed at closing?

You will want to have these items complete or in hand when you come to the closing (please confirm with your escrow officer, as practices vary by state):

Buyer

Buyer's copy of purchase agreement
Cashier's check(s) or collected funds to make all payments
Proof of purchase of insurance for fire, casualty, etc.
Invoices for any items to be paid at closing on behalf of the Buyer
Photo identification (passport, driver's license, or state-issued identification card)
Proof of a valid Social Security or Tax ID number

Seller

Seller's copy of purchase agreement
Invoices for any items to be paid at closing on behalf of the Seller
Receipts for last payment of interest on mortgages
Any unrecorded instruments that affect the title
Proof of satisfaction of any mechanics' liens, chattel mortgages, judgments, or mortgages that were paid prior to the closing
Photo identification (passport, driver's license, or state-issued identification card)
Proof of a valid Social Security or Tax ID number

Can my title company handle the closing?

Yes, in most areas of the country. Title insurance companies and/or title agents act as a central clearinghouse for the parties involved—collecting necessary documents, insuring adherence to the lender's title instructions, making arrangements for proper payment and distribution of funds. We are fully prepared to work with you from the beginning of your transaction all the way through to conclusion.

Should I shop around for the best Title Insurance deal?

Some states closely regulate rates. Others permit open competition, often resulting in significant differences between title insurers on rates and coverage. Depending where you live, it pays to investigate your options carefully in order to obtain the most complete coverage.

How much does Title Insurance cost?

The one-time premium is directly related to the value of your home. Typically, it is less expensive than your annual auto insurance. It is a one-time only expense, paid when you purchase your home. Yet it continues to provide complete coverage for as long as you or your heirs own the property.

When should I look into purchasing Title Insurance?

Call Getty Abstract & Title Company as soon as you and the seller sign the purchase agreement. With a brief summary of the details, our team of title experts will begin a search of the public records and issue a title commitment. Because there are a number of steps we must take to make certain that we know all we can about the title, it is wise to get the ball rolling as soon as possible.

But the lender already requires Title Insurance; won't that protect me?

Not necessarily. There are two types of Title Insurance. Your lender will likely require that you purchase a Lender's Policy. This policy only insures that the financial institution has a valid, enforceable lien on the property. Most lenders require this type of insurance, and typically require the borrower to pay for it.

An Owner's Policy on the other hand is designed to protect you from title defects that existed prior to the issue date of your policy. Title troubles, such as improper estate proceedings or pending legal action, could put your equity at serious risk. If a valid claim is filed, in addition to financial loss up to the face amount of the policy, your owner's title policy covers the full cost of any legal defense of your title.

The purchase of a real estate property is a life altering event. Please let us make sure it is not only a positive experience, but also one that you have fun with. Knowing you have worked with experienced professionals who accomplished everything that needed to be done in a timely and orderly manner will make the entire process less stressful and efficient.

First
Bank &
Trust

Brian R. Spaans
Mortgage Loan Officer
First Bank & Trust
2300 W. 57th Street
Sioux Falls SD 57108
ph.605-782-8080
www.bankeasy.com
brian.spaans@bankeasy.com

With over 10 years in the banking industry and a proud loan officer with First Bank & Trust I am deeply honored and very proud to be a part of this unprecedented book with The Messerschmidt Team. They are a real estate team that I have had the pleasure of getting to know through our work together and they are true professionals as well as great people who focus on the success of the customers and the integrity with which they conduct their business.

It is my passion and my profession to provide the highest level of service to everyone I work with and conduct myself with the utmost integrity in every area of my life. I have created three cornerstones to my career which include a service attitude, integrity and customer education.

I work every single day to develop in a greater way a spirit of service to everyone I come into contact with. This goes for all of my clients as well as anyone I meet and greet throughout my day. I attend many educational development courses, review and progressively grow all of the basic skills vital to my industry, and study numerous books that give me the extra knowledge that allows me to provide superior service.

It is my goal with this chapter to help you answer any questions you have regarding the mortgage process. An educated person is a powerful individual. Although I will answer many questions throughout this chapter, if you have any further questions, I want to invite you to contact me or stop into my office and I will be happy to answer any questions you have.

Common Mortgage Terms

I want to first start out by explaining common terms used throughout the mortgage process that may be slightly confusing. Here are a list of terms, their definitions and their functions.

Escrow: Escrow is an account established by First Bank & Trust, as your mortgage company, to pay property tax and insurance during the term of the mortgage. This keeps your payments level throughout the entire year. Escrow accounts also help you avoid having to pay extra for taxes and insurance. If you get compensated based on an hourly wage or you are salaried, this is a wonderful option for you.

If you decide you do not want to escrow, you must provide 20% down of you total investment. Because of this factor, most consumers choose to escrow.

Private Mortgage Insurance (PMI): PMI is designed to protect the lender from a loss if the borrower defaults on their loan and a foreclosure takes place.

For example, if a borrower purchases a home initially valued at $100,000 and then enters into foreclosure. When the bank seizes the property and it is only worth $90,000, the PMI will cover the difference in the amount.

Depending on your income bracket, PMI could be tax deductible to you.

Title Insurance: Title Insurance is put in place to protect the purchase of your home so you do not inherit any leans or outstanding bills owed associated with the property from the previous owner.

This insures that all previous contractors, mortgages, and subcontractors have been paid in full. Most often, this fee is split 50/50 by the buyer and seller.

There is no way to get around this cost when you are borrowing money; it is required. Title insurance is a one-time payment, unless you refinance your home.

Hazard Insurance: Otherwise known as home owners insurance. Hazard Insurance was created to protect your property against damage, fire, theft, wind, tornado, or any other unforeseen potential hazards to your home.

Closing: Closing is the end of the process in which you sign all required paperwork in order to purchase your new home. After this step is completed in its entirety, you get the keys!

Your closing will generally take place 30-45 days after you make an offer on the home. If you are required to put money down to complete the transaction, this is the time you would need to make the payment.

When working with me and The Messerschmidt team, we will be at the closing with you to assist in any way possible and be there for you to answer any questions you may have.

Your closing will take around one hour. This always is scheduled between 8AM and 4PM during typical business days so you will more than likely have to take time off from work to complete this final step.

Good Faith Estimate: I will provide this to you and it outlines the details of your transaction. Such as the terms, costs, your out of pocket obligations, and also what your mortgage payments will be.

It is important to keep in mind this is only an estimate. Variable factors can change throughout the process and it is not uncommon for me to create two or three Good Faith Estimates throughout the entire process for you. I will work extremely diligently to create an estimate that will be accurate for you and your family.

This allows you to compare your options to assure you are doing what is in your best interest. This is also a disclosure so you know what to expect. If you ask your lender for a Good Faith Estimate and they do not provide it, you absolutely must get a new lender, as this is a vital part of the home buying process for you.

I will always have these available to you so everyone knows exactly what is going on throughout the process.

Appraisal: A tool the banks use to make sure the home is worth at least what the home is being purchased for.

Appraisers are generally at the home for 10-15 minutes tops, at which time they will conduct a final walk through, take measurements, and double check everything. On occasion, there will be two people who will conduct this process. Banks take this step to assure all parties that there is nothing seriously wrong with the home.

Many people initially think this is the same as the general inspection and it will take several hours, but, as stated earlier, this will not take long at all.

This is required if you are financing your home and it is generally paid for by the buyer.

Underwriting: The process the bank uses to determine if the applicant qualifies for the product they are applying for or to assure the borrower meets or exceeds the minimum requirements needed to purchase the home.

The bank has a set of rules and regulations all borrowers must comply with in order to qualify. There is a list of guidelines which include debt to income ratio and credit. I will briefly explain both further.

Your *debt to income ratio* is defined as what percentage of your monthly gross income goes toward paying debt.

Banks generally do not want your existing monthly payments plus your new house payment to exceed 40% of your monthly gross income.

Debt to income ratio is pretty clear cut, but the *credit* aspect of this process can be relatively broad. The bank will analyze your credit to make sure a majority of payments have been made on time. Many times if the majority of payments have been made on time, you will be just fine. The only exception to this is your past mortgage payments. If you've been tardy within the last 12 months, it may be difficult for the lender to approve you for a loan.

I want you to understand there is not a magic score that will get you a yes or no. I will look at your overall credit to see if the payments have been paid on time and if this looks good, then I will be able to get you qualified with a product that is right for you.

It is not a major downfall, as popularly believed, to have late payments on your history. If you have a few minor late payments within the last couple of years, do not be discouraged to apply for a loan. I am willing to work with you.

What we consider to be a minor setback is when you have one or two small payments that have been missed within the last couple of years. If this is the case, you will have a great chance to still be approved.

This is where my knowledge and skills will come into play and be to your benefit, because every person's credit score is different. My knowledge and experience gives me an advantage to create the best scenario for all parties.

Do not let this phase of the process scare you. We will not pull your credit and instantly walk you out of the door or anything of the sort. I am passionate about educating you to help you improve your financial condition in any way possible.

Keep in mind, we want your business. Even if it doesn't happen right away, we will assist you in improving your credit as much as possible. Sometimes there may be a circumstance that can be fixed in a month and I am able to help people get in their dream home responsibly and effectively.

What to Expect From Beginning to End

The first step is to have an initial one hour meeting with me. It is recommended to have this session even before you find the home you want to purchase.

In this meeting, we will cover how much you may put down initially, what payments you could expect, and I will write you a good faith estimate. If you meet with a lender for an initial meeting of this kind and the length of the meeting is less than 50 minutes, to be honest, your lender is not doing a good enough job for you. This is an important meeting and will help you save time on the back end of the process.

After this session, you will have a good idea as far as what to expect and the next steps to be taken. You will also have an idea of what you are approved for. I will conduct the application during this time. Also, I can usually do the underwriting at this time.

After we conduct this first meeting and you are comfortable with everything, you will then go back to The Messerschmidt Team to find your dream home.

I want you to know, when you are working with me, the timeline as to when these steps are taken is completely up to you and your comfort level. This could happen in as little as a few hours or it could be several months. I make sure my clients are in the driver's seat as much as possible.

After you find the best house for you and your family, I want so suggest something slightly different that will give you an edge and could potentially save you time and money. I strongly recommend, when you find the right home, to call me back again so I can write another good faith estimate on the specific property. I suggest this because at this point I can now add to the final number insurance options, taxes, and will have a better idea of what you payment should be. Using my experience and knowledge, I can estimate within $15 as to what your monthly payment will be and know within a couple hundred dollars what you will need for closing.

At this point, the variable is with your insurance. Once this is figured out you will have a very clear idea of what to expect. To aid my clients, I have arranged a unique environment where I can get an insurance quote within 15 minutes. This is an exclusive service only available through my office at this time. I am the only service in Sioux Falls that gives you the opportunity to have the insurance representative, lender, and real estate team literally under one roof. This saves immensely in time, money, and headaches.

With this convenience, you will not have to schedule several different appointments in different locations around town, which is a major benefit to anyone, especially if you are from out of town. This also eliminates any communication gaps that occur when all three entities are at separate locations.

It is also important for you to understand that myself, our insurance provider, and The Messerschmidt Team, although under one roof, are still independent companies. We are not collaborating to make the most profit, but to save you the most time and money as well as provide the best service in the area.

After I have written an accurate Good Faith Estimate, it is time to schedule the appraiser and the closing time, and to make sure the insurance bill is prepared. You will see why it is so critical to have everyone under one roof at this point.

If you are a first time homebuyer and you don't want to rush into anything without consulting with me first, I have put my cell phone on my card. More often than not, you will make your offer on the home you want after regular business hours or on the weekend because that's when you have time to do it, and for this reason I make myself highly available from my virtual and home offices so I can tell you in minutes what the payments will be on that home before you make the offer.

With this knowledge, you can then go back with even more confidence and write the offer. Once the offer has been accepted, you will provide me with a copy of the purchase agreement and then I can lock the interest rate for you at the lowest possible rate available.

After the interest rate has been locked, you can then get the home inspection, which usually takes two to three business days from the time the offer is accepted to get the inspection done. Then, I will order the appraisal, which is done within a week.

As you can see, this is a very complicated process with many steps and variables. Anytime during this process you can feel free to stop into my office or call me directly with any questions or concerns. I will make myself available to you so the end outcome is you getting the keys to your dream home.

What will save me the most time?

The aspect that saves you the most time is working with an experienced professional who is prepared and can help you come to the first meeting as prepared as possible. I always help my clients come to the meetings fully prepared so we can maximize the time we spend working together.

I will ask you to bring your last two years in tax returns, a copy of a recent pay stub (if this applies to you), as well as a copy of a recent bank statement. If you bring these items with you to the initial meeting, everything will be much easier and there is a good chance you will leave knowing what you are approved for.

If you want to save the most time, it is best to get this initial meeting done right away. This will literally save you hours on the back end. It will also save you from worrying about the late payment you made two years ago for the Plasma T.V. you bought at Best Buy, which isn't a big deal, but many people let these worries stop them from proceeding to get their perfect home.

This will probably be the single most expensive item you buy in your entire life, and will require extra planning, especially if this is your first time through the entire process. Always remember, I will be working with you every step of the way, so you will not feel left behind or in a state of confusion.

If you get the wrong car, things can be done to easily fix that purchase. If you get into the wrong mortgage, this could cost you thousands of dollars to get things straightened out, so it is absolutely crucial to make sure you and your lender are thoroughly prepared. I will even help you outline your monthly budget so you know exactly what you can or cannot afford.

I want to reiterate the importance of coming into my office for the initial meeting before you start looking for homes. It is not only important to know what you are qualified for and can afford before looking for homes—it is vital. This is because purchasing a home is an emotional decision. You must be able to logically justify your purchase by knowing exactly what you can and cannot afford. The Messerschmidt Team and I will get you into the home that you truly want, and when you get the keys, you will have peace of mind knowing it is the right decision financially as well as emotionally.

How do I choose the right lender for me?

I want to strongly suggest that you work with a local bank that is rooted in strong family and business values such as First Bank & Trust. Do not work through internet lenders or 800-numbers and put yourself in a situation where you will never actually meet the lender, because this will put you at a major disadvantage throughout the process.

Meet with the potential lender face to face and be sure you ask for an in-person meeting upfront. Some lenders are not willing to meet with people right away and this is an example of a lender not dedicated to providing the best service. The absolute minimum to meet with your lender is once during the process. Make sure they are not only good at their profession, but are working with a reputable company as well. This is why I encourage you to come into my office any time and I will make time available for you to get educated and organized.

A good bank and loan officer will be flexible and adapt to your hours. Whether meeting at 5:30 or 6:00 P.M. or Saturday mornings, I recognize this is a significant purchase, so I will try to make the process as smooth as possible.

Another absolute must is to have someone sit down and to explain the Good Faith Estimate and how everything is working. If they are not willing to do this, find someone else.

I suggest asking your realtor for recommendations of who they feel is the best choice due to the fact that they deal with lenders on a daily basis and thus will have a better idea as to who is effective and who is not. Your friend may have one experience that was good or bad, but the next person will have had a different experience, which will create an entirely different impression, so ask a professional from the industry as to what their opinion is.

The bottom line is to work with someone who clearly demonstrates, by action and results, that they are dedicated to outstanding customer service, committed to building a relationship with their clients, and operate with complete and total integrity, regardless of the situation or who they are dealing with. These are the characteristics that have become my standard of performance. I take great pride in watching people get their dream homes and knowing it was a wise investment that will benefit them years to come.

Call today to schedule your initial session with me and to receive a free budget analysis brochure.

Industry Experts

Mark Madeja
Insurance Sales Manager for AAA South Dakota
Offices located at:
1300 Industrial Ave (across from the Arena)
605-336-3690
3701 W. 49th St. Suite 100 (49th & Louise)
605-361-2107
Toll free at 800-786-8322

Security and Peace of Mind

Many companies sell insurance, but at AAA, we prefer to develop lifelong member relationships by discussing your needs, lifestyle, and long-term goals. We then tailor an insurance plan specific to you. It's business the old fashioned way; what you should expect from someone who's been around since 1902. In South Dakota, we've been delivering service and value since 1925, and with almost 89,000 members state wide, we don't take our commitment to you lightly.

AAA Insurance has been in business over 90 years, is on the A.M. Best A+ Superior rating list, and has over 2.5 billion dollars in written premium, making it one of the largest Insurance Companies in the U.S. Through the collaborative efforts of AAA clubs nationwide, this represents value added member benefits, bringing you the highest levels of protection at the lowest possible cost.

Now, let's talk homeowners insurance . . . one of the reasons you're reading this book. The time to understand your Insurance policy is before a loss occurs, not afterwards. Our desire is to educate you, here and now, on what you need to know prior to making the investment of a lifetime: the purchase of your home.

"Your service has been nothing short of impressive. I get immediate and professional responses whether I call or e-mail. If my Agent doesn't know the answer, she/he takes the time to research it and get back to me promptly with accurate information. Even though I live outside of Sioux Falls, there has never been a disconnect in service levels. And on top of that, you saved me money over my prior carrier!"
Wayne Beck

Insurance Value

The purchase price of a home and the replacement price of a home (or the amount the home is actually insured for) are often two different numbers, and can easily be a place of confusion for the homeowner. Remember, however, that purchase price is a result of current market conditions, whereas replacement price is based upon each and every piece of material needed to restore your home exactly as it was prior to a loss.) Our job as insurance professionals is not only to make sure we have your home insured correctly should we have to rebuild it, but also to ensure we can replace everything inside your home.

We determine the correct replacement cost of your home based on square footage, features, architectural style, custom amenities, attached and detached structures, etc. A good insurance policy usually protects the home at between 125-150% of its replacement value, thus allowing for spikes in material costs or availability in the event of a loss.

Be a savvy shopper. Each insurance company has its own underwriting criteria and guidelines. Many factors can be involved in determining the price of your new homeowners' policy: inside or outside city limits, acreage, wood shake or asphalt shingles, swimming pools, trampolines, and so on. At AAA, we strive to meet the needs of each member; thus, our insurance policies, being individually risk based, allow a wide range of acceptable profiles.

Home Policies

A home policy is essentially split into two sections: Property protection and Liability protection.

Property protection is specific to your home, the contents within it, and other real property improvements such as patios, gazebos, fences, etc. In addition to replacement value coverage on your home, insist on replacement value (and not actual cash value) for the contents of your home. Essentially, it's the difference between settling a claim at retail prices versus wholesale prices.

Items such as antiques, jewelry, and firearms are typically not covered beyond a nominal maximum amount, and thus will need to be scheduled on your policy to reflect the replacement value of those items. Typically, the additional cost is based on a dollar amount per hundred or per thousand, and most scheduled items are not subject to a deductible. Remember to list, photograph, or videotape everything in your home and store it somewhere secure. Should a claim occur, you'll be eternally grateful you did.

Liability protection is exactly that—anything you may become liable for, and is typically broken into two parts: Personal Liability and Medical Payments. Personal Liability provides coverage against a claim or lawsuit resulting from bodily injury or property damage to others caused by an accident on your property or as a result of personal activities anywhere. This coverage protects you and all family members who live with you. The Medical Payments section includes coverage to pay medical expenses for persons accidentally injured on your property regardless of fault. Typically liability coverage also includes the cost of legal defense, up to the limits of your policy. Increased liability coverage is dirt cheap when purchased as part of your home policy. Always buy as much as the policy will allow you to. As with every homeowner's policy, certain exclusions apply. Read the fine print!

Umbrella Policy

Every home and automobile policy has a maximum limit of coverage. To protect against ever experiencing a situation where those limits would be insufficient, an umbrella policy can be purchased (quite reasonably) to "cover" you in the event of a catastrophe. An umbrella policy is usually sold as an endorsement to your homeowners' policy. You choose the amount of coverage you deem necessary, typically 1 to 5 million dollars.

Obviously, we've only skimmed the surface of the subject of you and your home owners insurance, but we'd welcome the opportunity to discuss your individual insurance needs and answer any other questions you may have!

"I wanted to let you know how much I appreciate your hard efforts, honesty, sincere interest in finding the best programs or policies to fit our needs and budget. You truly listened and delivered without going for more than what we needed. You also have one heck of a sense of humor that makes it comfortable to work with you."
Matt and Karen Harsh

Contact us today for a professional no-obligation analysis of your insurance needs at one of our two Sioux Falls offices. Get more . . . get AAA!

Charlie Azzara
Founder, Co-Owner, Tax Consultant—Azzara Tax Service
Phone: (605) 335-4983 www.azzaratax.com

Azzara Tax Service is a full time tax preparation firm serving all of the immediate and surrounding areas of Sioux Falls, SD. Our newly located South-Sioux Falls offices are located on the lower level of the Ameri-star Real Estate building.

We have an incredible staff that is dedicated to providing our clients with quality, timely service so we can get you the best possible tax return. We continue to loyally serve our existing clients, and we welcome those new to us who desire better performance from their tax service.

When you work with our office, we work with a very hands-on approach. You are able to sit down with us and you have the option to actually watch us work on your tax preparation. With this approach, you are able to ask us questions as we work on getting you the best tax return possible. We have found our clients enjoy and appreciate this service option.

We will ask you certain questions to help identify areas where we will be able to uncover other deductions you may not have been aware of. And, if you get audited, we will be there to help you work with the IRS so the process will be as stress free as possible.

Home Ownership Tax Benefits

Now that you are living the American Dream through home ownership, you can enjoy your new home and also all the tax benefits that come with it. However, to take full advantage of the home of your dreams, your tax preparation process may become slightly more complicated than before ownership, and this is why it is vitally important to work with professional tax consultants like our staff at Azzara Tax Service.

We will now briefly explain and highlight some main tax deductions that could be available to you now that you own your home.

1.) Points

Throughout the mortgage process, your lender will charge a various amount of fees, one of these fees is called "points." One point equals 1% of the loan principal. It is not uncommon to have one or two points on your home loan, which could add up to thousands of dollars. There are ways you can fully deduct these points, although not all at once, but this is a deduction option for you.

2.) Mortgage Interest

You could have the possibility to deduct some of the interest you pay on your home equity loan or credit line. The IRS will, however, place a limit on the amount of your debt that can be treated as "home equity" for the deduction.

3.) Interest on Loans for Home Improvement

If you receive a loan to make substantial improvements to your home, you have the opportunity to possibly deduct that interest, without a specific dollar limit. The improvement must be capital improvement, however, and not just ordinary repairs.

4.) Property Taxes

Your property taxes are completely deductible from your income. As with all of these deductions, there is a definite protocol that must be followed which is why it is essential to work with us and we will help you make all the proper deductions.

5.) Home Office Deduction

If you have a home office, you may be able to deduct home costs that are directly related to that portion of the home. Some options for deduction could be costs for repairs, insurance and depreciation.

Always keep in mind the IRS favors real estate investments, which makes real estate a financially solid investment for anyone who is looking for tax benefits as well as high long-term return on investment.

Call us today at 335-4983 and let us help you get the best possible return for you and your family.

Closet Pros, Inc.

Let the Pros Help You Organize!

Eric Boysen
Owner
(605) 360-8287
eboysen@sio.midco.net

"Eric designed, constructed, and installed all of the closets at my lake home. I am thrilled with how they turned out. Every closet suits the person it was designed for. I find myself leaving the closet doors open!"
Penny Paclik

An uncluttered home is a peaceful home

If you are looking to get more organized and experience the feeling of calmness that comes with having a custom closet design, you are not alone. Countless homeowners are seeking out professionals such as Closet Pros, Inc. to organize their home and garage to gain a new feeling of organization and order in their life.

Not only does a custom closet design give you a feeling of relaxation in your home, it also can significantly raise the real estate market value of your home.

Wardrobes are getting larger than ever. Individuals and families 50 years ago were content with an average wardrobe consisting of every day garments and clothing with only a select few pieces of special occasion clothing.

Today, we are much more fashion conscious. We not only have an abundant supply of clothing for all occasions, but we also have many different kinds and designs of accessories as well. With all the various styles, types, and volume of clothing, it is more important than ever to have a custom design for your closet and garage.

Simply put, the more organized you are, the more peaceful and calm you will be throughout your days.

Organization is the target and calmness is the feeling

With our custom closet design platform, you are able to work with one person throughout the entire creation, design, manufacture, and installation of your own custom closet. We take custom design to a new level with our CAD software application, which will give you a clear picture of exactly what your new closet with look like in your home. With this tool, you are able to mix and match colors, drawers, and hanging space to assure you that your closet will look exactly how you want it to look.

No other company in the Sioux Falls area will be able to give you the one-on-one attention than I will do with you. I will work with you, directly, through every step of the process from start to finish. This way you won't have to contact a customer support representative who may not have even seen your closet design or whose expertise exists in other areas of the industry. Another major benefit you receive when working with me is I have the option to use a furniture melamine grade product, which will increase the value of your home considerably and add a feeling of total luxury in your closet.

I will create your design in such a way that it will be totally adjustable for you and can be easily changed in the future. Your closet design wants and needs today will be totally different five years from now as your lifestyle changes and your family grows. With my methods of design and implementation, you won't have to worry about remaking everything in a few years. I will continue to work with you to as your needs change and expand.

The Closet Pro Process

When I come into your home, I have a system that I will follow to guarantee your satisfaction. The first thing I do is sit with you and your family to assess and quantify all of your specific wants and needs. I have a list of questions that I ask to really gain an understanding of what you are looking for with your design.

I use a special software application that has been exclusively created for closet design. Using my software, I am able to get everything done much quicker, accurately, and with more efficiency, which in turn saves you time and money. This application also allows me to take any guesswork out of the process for you so you will always be informed on what is happening with your closet designs.

Once I know precisely what you want, I will put all of the gathered data into the program and create a printed drawling so you can see exactly what you are getting.

Something that all of my clients love to see are the 3-D images I create for them to see exactly how everything will look before I actually install the closets. This is a fun time for my clients.

It is important to understand that the design for your new closet must be done using software. Many companies use hand drawings, which will actually reduce the accuracy of the measurements and could cause potential problems in the implementation phase.

Whether we work on your closet or your garage storage, professional design will raise the value of your property and make it actually look bigger in the mind of a buyer.

When your home is less cluttered and more organized, your home will also show better and be a more relaxing environment for you and your family to live and grow in.

Call me today at (605) 360-8287 to schedule your free consultation!

"I have worked with Eric for over 3 years. He works directly with my customers and takes into account their needs and budget to come up with a great organization plan that really works."

James Benning

Home Warranty, Inc.
www.homewarrantyinc.com
Phone: 877-977-4949

This could save you thousands of dollars

Did you know your homeowners insurance does not cover repairs and replacements due to "wear and tear," but a Home Protection Plan from Home Warranty, Inc. does? Our Home Protection Plans ensure that the appliances and mechanical systems of your home are maintained in working order long after the closing.

A home warranty is a service contract that covers the repairs and replacements necessary to restore the appliances and mechanical systems of your home to normal operating conditions. You are able to call one toll-free number and we send a service technician out to take care of the problem.

Our standard Home Protection Plan covers the heating system, central air conditioner, air exchanger, ductwork, interior plumbing, interior electrical wiring, water heater, sump pump, central vacuum, garage door openers, garbage disposal, trash compactor, built-in microwave oven, range/oven/cook top, dishwasher, refrigerator, washer, and dryer.

Understand that not all home warranties are created equal. We give you the choice of using your own service provider. We give you the choice of applying the repair estimate towards replacement. Plus, unlike most other warranty plans, our standard coverage does not set predetermined dollar limits on your most expensive items.

"We bought an older home a few years back and have had to use our warranty several, times as our furnace and air conditioning units were reaching the end of their useful life. Home Warranty, Inc. has already provided prompt, friendly service and the option to use my repair money towards a replacement appliance is awesome!"
Beth F.

Sell your home for more money!

Every study conducted has shown that home warranties sell homes faster and for more money. The warranty gives the buyer confidence to purchase your home without fear of costly repairs after the sale, and the money a buyer would normally keep back in anticipation of future repairs is freed up to use in negotiations on your property. Many times, the Home Protection Plan from Home Warranty, Inc. can mean the difference between someone making an offer on your home or passing on it altogether. After all, if someone doesn't come to the table to make an offer, you can't sell them your home.

Our Home Protection Plan:

· Sells homes faster, for more money, and gives them a better chance of selling at all.
· Can be used with *no risk* of having to pay for the plan if you don't get the price you are looking for on your home.
· Has no payment due until the close of sale.
· Offers you great liability protection after the sale of your home.
· Offers optional heating and air coverage for you during the listing period for a small fee.
· Covers nearly 35 appliances and mechanical systems.

Save Yourself Thousands of Dollars

Our protection plan protects you against costly repairs or replacements of appliances and mechanical systems for one year after buying your home. If you're like most home buyers, a new furnace or other large repair doesn't fit in with your plans for a new home.

The Home Protection Plan from Home Warranty, Inc.:

· Covers nearly 35 appliances and mechanical systems. You can view a list on our website listed at www.homewarrantyinc.com
· Comprehensive replacement or repairs of covered items are taken care of by making a simple phone call to **Home Warranty, Inc**.
· Uses trusted local contractors for all repairs.
· Provides cash payments for replacements or in lieu of repairs so you can upgrade to the appliance of your choice.
· Only a small $75 trade service fee per incident and **Home Warranty, Inc.** pays the rest of the covered repair.

Call Home Warranty, Inc. today at 877-977-4949 and *really* protect your investments!

"We sold our home during the winter and figured we would try using a home warranty to hopefully help the property sell faster and attract more buyers. We didn't realize we would also have coverage for ourselves during the time the home was on the market. We ended up having work done during that time that would have complicated matters during the listing. We are so thankful we put the warranty in place. It definitely helped sell our home."
Mark K.

Jerry Berg
Owner
www.intekclean.com
800-456-5004

"Once again INTEK has made the carpet in my home look like new! The two young men who came into my home were exceptionally thorough."
Tammy

In 1984, I started a small business designed to provide cleaning services to customers in the Sioux Falls area. Now INTEK has grown in to a full-service, professional cleaning and restoration company serving both residential and commercial customers.

Since the beginning, INTEK has provided prompt and courteous service to all of our customers. We understand your need for deep cleaning and we genuinely care about providing you with top-quality service at a reasonable price. We have developed a loyal clientele who regularly rely on our cleaning services. Businesses and homeowners—both longtime and first-time clients—depend on us, and we remain true to our commitments.

The foundation of my business is our commitment to service excellence. Many companies make commitments, but only hold them when it is convenient. Our commitments are independent of circumstances and do not change when circumstances are altered. We make sure we are very direct on what we will deliver to you and we will follow through with our commitments. Below, I will outline a short list of the many services we offer you and commit to completion.

Carpet Cleaning

We have been voted #1 by the *Local Best* by customers in the community for our carpet cleaning services! Our professionally trained technicians are here to assist in improving and maintaining the beauty of your home. As always, **INTEK** maintains our professionalism with each carpet technician in full uniform complete with identification badges.

Furnace and Duct Cleaning

Did you know that furnace and duct cleaning could be the healthiest home improvement you will ever make? Having your ducts cleaned eliminates dust, pet hair, pollen, mold, and other irritants from your furnace and ductwork, and at the same time increases the efficiency of your home energy system. If you suffer from allergies, cleaning your ductwork could improve your situation.

Building a new home? Often times with new constructions, debris such as sheetrock, wrappers, screws, nails, and sawdust can drop into your ductwork.

At **INTEK**, we offer a **free video inspection** of your ductwork so you can decide whether or not you feel our services are necessary. This service has proven to be invaluable, and we are proud to offer dryer vent cleaning services.

Mold Remediation

Our experienced Mold Remediation professionals set up containment units to make sure the mold spores are confined to the containment area. Negative air pressurization is utilized to keep the spores isolated within the containment area to prevent crosscontamination. The air in the containment area is then filtered through our **H.E.P.A.** air scrubber units and safely dispersed outside your home. Upon completion of the mold remediation project, the area is tested by an outside firm to make sure the mold spore count is back to an acceptable level for occupancy. Once air quality is approved, our professionals then restore the area back to its original condition.

Fire Damage Restoration

We understand the distress and confusion that follow a fire. We've lived through countless situations like this with our customers, and we work hard to help ease the burden by handling the loss. In these scenarios we handle all the needs of the customer by working with the adjusters, insurance companies, submitting detailed estimates and following through with these estimates.

Our professionally trained staff is experienced in restoring your property after it has been damaged by fire or smoke. We have many years of experience with both commercial and residential losses.

"It was sheer joy to walk in the lumber yard last Sunday morning and see the floors shining like a million dollars!! You did a terrific job and we THANK YOU SO MUCH for your hard work!!"
Wendell & Betty Ames

Call us today at 800-456-5004 to ask any questions you have or to schedule an appointment!

Mike Hartman
Owner—Radon Mitigation Systems, LLC
www.RadonMitigationSystems.com
Phone: (605) 261-4440
ClientCare@RadonMitigationSystems.com

"Radon Mitigation Systems came to my house, gave me a bid and installed the system all within 24 hours! They are very fast, very courteous and explained how the system works in a very simple, easy to understand manner. I'd recommend them to anyone who wants a safer home for their family."
Laura Minnick

Radon Mitigation Systems, LLC is one of only a handful of EPA-approved radon mitigation firms in the entire State of South Dakota. This means that we are held to a higher standard—one that's good for you and the health of your loved ones.

Our work is guaranteed. We believe in providing you with the best equipment and the best installation for your home. Each system is specifically designed to best suit your home. The final product looks clean, neat, and, more importantly, it works properly to offer you peace of mind.

We work with homeowners, Realtors, and home inspectors. We know that when you're trying to sell your home, a "clean bill of health" makes your property sell faster and presents fewer hassles. We also understand that timing is everything when your home is on the market. Your health and safety is a sign of our success, and we pride ourselves on maintaining a high level of service and support to all our clients.

Owner of Radon Mitigation Systems, Mike Hartman, grew up right in the heart of Sioux Falls. Mike graduated from Lincoln High School and joined the Air Force as an aircraft mechanic. He became licensed through the Federal Aviation Administration (FAA) before retiring in 1999. He continued his success working for Toyota, where he oversaw over one hundred workers and was awarded Manager of the Year, then moved back to his roots to be closer to his family in Sioux Falls. He is excited to be serving the Sioux Falls community with such an important and lifesaving service to offer.

As you read this, you may be asking a very common question: "*What is radon?*" It is important to understand that radon is a naturally occurring, colorless, odorless, highly radioactive gas. It is produced by the natural radioactive decay of uranium 238 in rock, soil, and water. Radon and its associated by-products emit alpha and beta particles and gamma rays. These particles attach themselves to other airborne particles such as dust, and are inhaled into your lungs. Once inside your lungs, they lodge in the mucus membranes. **The damage from these particles can cause cancer.**

Radon is the leading cause of lung cancer among non-smokers, and it is the second leading cause of lung cancer in America. Radon claims about 21,000 lives annually. The amount of Radon and the length of time you have been exposed to it determine your lung cancer risk from this sometimes-deadly gas. The higher the level, the higher the risk—it's just that simple.

It is impossible to predict radon levels in your home based on state or local levels. Testing is the only way to find out what your home's radon level is. We use a third party to conduct radon testing. This eliminates any potential conflict of interest. Once you've determined that the radon level in your home is above the EPA acceptable limit, feel free to call us for a free, in-home estimate with no obligation.

You can learn more about Radon mitigation and how these services relate to your Radon problem at our website, www.RadonMitigationSystems.com. The following is a list the primary services we offer:

- Conduct a pre-inspection
- Design a custom system to suit house
- Install and seal your sump pit with a cover
- Install a system routed above roofline
- Install a pump in the attic, garage, or exterior of your home
- Seal cracks and extrusions as needed
- Conduct a post mitigation inspection for leaks
- Test for back draft
- Install a manometer
- Wire the system with a licensed electrician

"We were very impressed with Radon Mitigation Systems. They answered all of our questions and installed a radon reduction system that reduced our home's radon level to a safe level. We were also impressed, while we were getting bids, that they are certified by the EPA. None of the other companies that we interviewed had any sort of certification."
Denise Dexter

Call us today to schedule a free inspection and estimate at (605) 261-4440.

Kim Thormodsgard
Owner—Thor Home Inspection Services
This Finest in Inspector Services
(605) 335-6889
www.thorhome.com
thorhome1@sio.midco.net

*"I was new to the area and not sure whom I could count on to do a home inspection.
Thor Home Inspection did a thorough job looking at the house and pointed out both
good and bad features. It was comforting to know I was getting an unbiased and
knowledgeable opinion during the hectic time of buying a new home."*
Lynn M. Kalisz

Buying a home or building is probably the biggest investment you'll ever make. This is a decision that will affect you for years to come, and the process can be extremely stressful and confusing. Of course, there is always considerable risk involved when you are making such a large purchase. A professional inspection will significantly reduce your risk and help make the entire home buying process easier and less stressful. The staff at Thor Home Inspection Services truly enjoys helping clients. Throughout the process, customer service is our highest priority.

Thor Home Inspection Services is a locally owned business that opened in 1996. We specialize in both residential and commercial inspection services. Our mission is clear: to provide the best service to our customers and to help them protect and maintain one of the most important investments they will ever make.

Kim Thormodsgard is the president and owner of Thor Home Inspection Services and has been a home and building inspector in the Sioux Falls area for over 13 years. Kim graduated with *highest honors* from NRI Schools in Washington, DC in 1996. NRI is accredited by the Commission of the National Home Study Council. Since graduation, he has attended numerous inspection seminars in Minneapolis, MN,; Omaha, NE; Orlando, Fla; and Sioux Falls, SD; compiling hundreds of hours of education. Kim has passed the U.S. EPA Radon Measurement Operator Course and the U.S. Department of

Housing and Urban Development Lead Hazard Visual Assessment Course. He has a long history of experience in single and multi-family housing construction. Kim has a suite of credentials and memberships, which include being a South Dakota State Licensed Home Inspector, a National Association of Certified Home Inspector, a candidate for the American Society of Home Inspectors, a member of the Foundation of Real Estate Appraisers & Inspectors, has a Residential Building Contractors License, a member of the Better Business Bureau, an affiliate member of the Realtor's Association of the Sioux Empire, and a member of the Sioux Falls Board of Historical Preservation.

Here are some common questions our clients have about home inspections along with our answers, based on our years of experience:

"What is a home inspection?"

A home inspection is a professional, complete visual examination of the all the systems and physical structural elements of a home. Our emphasis is on identifying existing or potential problems that would affect a purchaser's buying decision.

"Why do I need a home inspection?"

A home is the largest purchase most people will ever make. It only makes sense to find out as much as you can about the house you are interested in before you buy. With a professional inspection, you can avoid costly surprise repairs and problems with your new home and acquire advice to help you keep your home in top condition. If you are listing your home, you absolutely must have an inspection prior to the listing to avoid the buyer's inspector finding problems unknown to you that could suspend the purchase and cost you thousands of dollars.

"What does a home inspection include?"

Our standard inspection report covers all the major systems and structural elements of the house. This includes the condition of the home's heating and air conditioning systems, plumbing and electrical systems, roof, foundation, attic and visible insulation, walls, doors, windows, and all visible components.

When done correctly, a quick and thorough home inspection from Thor Home Inspection Services could not only save you thousands of dollars, but could also give you the peace of mind that your home is in top condition and the understanding to make sure it stays that way. Call Kim at (605) 521-9327 today to schedule an initial consultation and ask any questions you may have.

"I appreciated the professional and down to earth manner of Thor Home Inspection Service. The inspection was well worth the time and money spent for what I gained in concessions from the seller and for the knowledge I now have of my new residence."
Robyn L. Schmuck

Work Cited

Page 18
Robert Frost: American Poet, 1874-1963
http://thinkexist.com/quotation/the_best_way_out_is_always_through/149350.html

Page 19
Albert Einstein: Physicist, won Nobel Prize for physics in 1921; 1879-1955
http://thinkexist.com/search/searchquotation.asp?search=%93Try+not+to+become+a
+man+of+success+but+a+man+of+value.%94

Page 21
Vince Lombardi: Football Coach, world renowned for will power, strength and
determination; 1913-1970
http://thinkexist.com/search/searchquotation.asp?search=%93The+difference+betwee
n+a+successful+person+and+others+is+not+a+lack+of+strength%2C+not

Page 24
Martin Luther King Jr.: Baptist Minister; Civil Rights Leader; 1929-1968
http://thinkexist.com/quotation/the_time_is_always_right_to_do_what_is_right/8112.
html

Page 24
Confucius: Famous Chinese philosopher, teacher and theorist; 551-479 BC
http://thinkexist.com/quotation/our_greatest_glory_is_not_in_never_falling_but_
in/171663.html

Page 27
Helen Keller: Author and teacher who was deaf and blind; 1880-1968
http://thinkexist.com/quotation/life_is_either_a_daring_adventure_or_
nothing-to/13581.html

Page 29
Ralph Waldo Emerson: Philosopher, essayist, poet; 1803-1882
http://www.inspirational-quotes.info/life-quotes.html

Page 30
Frank Lloyd Wright: American Architect; 1869-1959
http://www.quotationspage.com/quote/1959.html

Page 31
Helen Keller: Author and teacher who was deaf and blind; 1880-1968
http://thinkexist.com/quotation/alone_we_can_do_so_little-together_we_can_do_
    so/144236.html

Page 35
Yogi Berra: Major League baseball player; born 1925
http://www.goodreads.com/quotes/show/23616

Page 40
Theodore Roosevelt: 26th American President; 1858-1919
http://thinkexist.com/quotation/the_most_important_single_ingredient_in_the/225663.
    html

Page 41
Napoleon Bonaparte: Military and political leader of France; 1769-1821
http://www.brainyquote.com/quotes/quotes/n/napoleonbo106371.html

Page 47
Jim Rohn: Famous American speaker and author
http://thinkexist.com/quotation/time_is_more_value_than_money-you_can_get_
    more/295523.html

Page 48
Proverb Quote:
http://thinkexist.com/quotation/the_art_is_not_in_making_money-but_in_
    keeping/196608.html

www.ingramcontent.com/pod-product-compliance
Lightning Source LLC
Chambersburg PA
CBHW022126170526
45157CB00004B/1776